RUSSIAN

Language and people

Written by
Terry Culhane
Produced by
Terry Doyle

BRITISH BROADCASTING CORPORATION

This book accompanies the BBC Continuing Education
television programmes *Russian Language and People*
First broadcast Spring 1980

Series produced by Terry Doyle

Published to accompany a series of
programmes in consultation with the
BBC Continuing Education Advisory Council

This book is set in Monotype
Times New Roman 10/12 pt.

First published 1980
Published by the British Broadcasting Corporation
35 Marylebone High Street, London W1M 4AA
Printed in England by William Clowes (Beccles) Limited
Beccles, Suffolk
ISBN 0 563 16303 8

Contents

Introduction

This course is designed to be a self-instructional introduction to the Russian language. It is based on skills of *understanding* rather than *speaking* Russian. Many of the exercises in the book and on the records/ cassettes are of a 'problem-solving' nature, involving the retrieval of information from Russian sources, both oral and visual. Timetables, menus, signs, press cuttings, maps and other source materials figure largely in the course and an attempt has been made to devise an approach which will be of practical use to the visitor to the Soviet Union, as well as being informative and of general interest.

Anyone who follows the course carefully should, by the end of it, be able to 'survive' linguistically in the Soviet Union, a society very different from our own. He should also learn something about the nature of Soviet society, and the situations he is likely to find himself in during a visit to the USSR although details, prices etc., are of course liable to change.

There are two major difficulties associated with starting to learn Russian. One is the alphabet, and the other is vocabulary. In this course the alphabet is presented gradually over the first five units (one unit = book chapter, plus corresponding sound recording), and the vocabulary introduced in these units consists mainly of words which look and sound like English, but are in frequent and current use in spoken and written Russian. The gradual introduction of the alphabet means that a few necessary words and expressions have been 'transliterated' (written in Latin characters) during the first four units.

How to use the book

First of all, the book does not contain everything that is in the television series. The two are constructed in parallel so that most of the vocabulary and structures occur in the same sequence, and the topics covered are the same. However, some students may wish to cover one unit a week, others may want to accelerate. Some may even fall behind! The self-instructional nature of the course is intended to cater for all these possibilities. So: proceed at your own pace, and do not give yourself unnecessary pressure. If you do accelerate, revise the appropriate unit before watching the television programme. You will find that this helps you consolidate what you have already absorbed.

Do not expect to understand every word or expression or grammatical form that you meet. If you ask the way to somewhere in simple language, you may receive a reply which is difficult to understand in

5

its entirety. This reply, however, will contain key words and expressions, the understanding of which will enable you to get to your destination. It is the object of this course to teach you simple ways of using Russian actively, and to provide you with enough understanding of the language to be able to decode more complex spoken and written Russian, by selecting the essential, relevant items.

There are very few complex grammatical terms used in the body of the text. Those which are used are explained in simple terms, either in the text or in the grammar notes at the end of the book. These grammar notes are mainly intended for the more academically minded reader — don't let them put you off! Use them if you find them useful, ignore them if you do not.

Each exercise is marked by a symbol in the margin. ☎ means that the exercise is recorded on the cassette or record; ◖ means that it is purely a reading or writing exercise. ▱ indicates exercises related to the alphabet (Record 1). Exercises which are recorded usually have a corresponding reading exercise for those who do not have the cassettes or records. The answers to the exercises are given in the back of the book, with a progress chart on which you can record your score and chart your progress, if you so wish.

Between Unit 5 and Unit 10 examples of written Russian are provided as aids to recognition. Writing exercises are provided from Unit 11 to Unit 15. These are optional. If you do not wish to learn to write Russian, but would like to be able to recognise written letters, you can do this by simply reading the exercises.

Each unit of the book has, at the end, a summary in English of the main points of the unit, together with a review of key words and phrases in Russian. This may be used as a progress check, as well as a quick reference point.

The cassettes and records

There are three records/cassettes designed for use in close conjunction with the book:

1   The Alphabet.
2   Exercises and dialogues.
3   Dialogues for repetition, and 'Moscow voices'.

You will learn more quickly and more effectively with the help of the recordings than without them.

In short, the aim of the course is to stimulate your interest in the Russian language and people, and to enable you to make a confident start in approaching them both. If you are able to work systematically through the book and sound recordings, as well as watch the television programmes, we feel sure you will have joined us in achieving this aim.

1
NOMER ODIN

Meeting people and naming things

See Grammar notes (Alphabet) page 152

Alphabet 1

The Russian alphabet is called Cyrillic after the missionary St. Cyril, who is thought by some to have devised it in the ninth century. It has some letters **комета** which look and sound very much like their English (Latin) counterparts. Some letters look like Latin letters but have different sounds. The ones in this group introduced here are **с** (s), **p** (r), **н** (n) and **в** (v). If you have come across the Greek alphabet you will guess that many of the Russian letters are derived from the Greek. A familiar example of this is the Russian **п** (p). Other letters are developed from Hebrew characters. Sometimes a single Russian letter constitutes a word, e.g. **и** (i) meaning 'and'.

One of the difficulties met by English speakers is the complex spelling which occurs when Russian words are written in English characters (when they are 'transliterated'). This is because two or more letters are often used in English to express a single letter in Russian. Once you have mastered the Russian sounds, this ceases to be a problem. The alphabet is introduced over the first five units in the course, a few letters at a time. English 'transliteration' will be used for words which contain letters which have not yet been taught. An approximate pronunciation guide will also be given, but of course pronunciation can only be learned properly by careful listening and by imitation of native speech. The cassettes and records accompanying the course contain listening and pronunciation exercises for this purpose. You will learn much more with the cassettes or records than without them, but, in any case, each time there is an exercise involving cassettes or records (marked ▄▄), a parallel reading exercise (marked ◖) will usually be included.

The words listed below are chosen because they are like English words, or because they are the sort of words which you may already know. All of them are common words in regular use in everyday Russian. There are two examples of abbreviation, which almost everyone will recognise — ТАСС (TASS), the Soviet news agency, and СССР (SSSR), the letters that represent USSR.

Letters you know	КОМЕТА
New letters	СПРИНВ

🔊 The words are recorded on your cassettes or records. On the first reading there is a gap for you to *repeat* the sound. On the second reading the gap occurs *before* the reading to enable you to *try out your own reading*. The correct version then follows for you to *check* your performance.

e.g. 1st reading   **nómer odín**   *number one*   комéта...GAP
                                                (REPEAT) ☐

                 nómer dva   etc.

   2nd reading   **nómer odín**   ...GAP
                             (READ)   комéта (CHECK) ☐

Place a tick in the box if you think you've got it right. Before you start, notice that the stresses have been marked on the words. Russian, like English, is stressed. The 'stressed' part of the word is where the stress or accent falls. This is *not* normally marked in Russian printed matter. It is included here to help you with pronunciation. Stress in Russian tends to be stronger than English stress, and may occur where you would not expect it (Nos. 5, 7, 11, 12, 13, 14, 15, 16). Try to get it right.

1	комéта	☐	8	óпера	☐	15	ресторáн	☐
2	ТАСС	☐	9	спорт	☐	16	оркéстр	☐
3	СССР	☐	10	парк	☐	17● áвиа	☐
4 ●	кáсса	☐	11	таксú	☐	18● мáрка	☐
5	теáтр	☐	12	пианúст	☐	19	нет	☐
6	áтом	☐	13	винó	☐	20	стоп	☐
7	метрó	☐	14● Москвá	☐			

● **кáсса** is a *cash-desk* or box-office. Every shop has one. It is also where you buy tickets for theatres, cinemas, museums, etc.

● **Москвá** *Moscow*. If you fly to Moscow it's probably the first word you'll see when you arrive at Sheremétevo, Moscow's international airport.

- **а́виа** means *Airmail*. You will see it printed on envelopes.
- **ма́рка** is a *stamp*. The USSR produces a large variety of stamps commemorating historical events, anniversaries and natural history.

If you are working without cassettes or records, turn to p. 153 for approximate pronunciation.

Don't worry about learning the words — simply try and remember the letters. You will meet the words frequently in the course. Notice that small letters are very similar to large ones.

There is no word for *a* in Russian, and none for *the*. This makes things simpler. Thus,

Éto teátr means *This is a theatre* or *This is the theatre*

Ya pianíst means *I am a pianist* or *I am the pianist*

On studént means *He is a student* or *He is the student*

You will notice from the above examples that there is no verb *to be*. This makes things even more simple!

The most important aim of this course is to help you to *understand* Russian. Most of the exercises will therefore concentrate on understanding the language rather than speaking it. The first exercise, however, is one of repetition.

1 👓 Look at the pictures below. You will be asked **shto eto?** 'What's this?' and you should reply '**eto**............'. The correct answer will then be given. If a person is involved, the question will be **kto eto?** '*Who's this?*'. The pictures are numbered to help you. The boxes are provided to enable you to check your answers. If you are not sure how to proceed, play the recording through. You will hear:
nomer...*number*...**shto éto?** [GAP]............**éto** _____ (Correct answer).

	Ex. 1	Ex. 2	Ex. 3
1			
2			
3			
4			
5			
6			
7			
8			
9			
10			

1

2

6

7

2 📼 This exercise requires negative answers. The Russian for *yes* is **da**, for *no* is **нет (nyet)** and for *not* is **не (nye)**. You will be asked '*Is this a _____?*' You should then answer '*No, it's not a _____, it's a _____*'. Again, if you're not sure what to do, play the recording. Check your answers in the boxes provided.

3 📼 Replay exercise 2. In each item the wrong object or person is identified in the first part. Find the appropriate picture and put its number in the box provided in the third column. Thus, if you hear '*No. 1 Is this a park?*', you would place 4 in the first box provided for exercise 3.

4 📖 Here is a jumbled list of the words indicated by the pictures below. Place the number of the appropriate picture in the box at the side of each word (*answers on p. 164*).

| оркéстр ☐ | винó ☐ | пáпа ☐ | таксѝ ☐ | ресторáн ☐ |
| парк ☐ | мáма ☐ | метрó ☐ | пианѝст ☐ | теáтр ☐ |

5 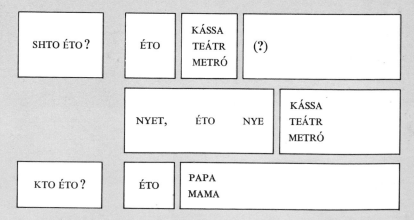 See if you can find the words in the square and fill in the blanks below. You can move in any direction, including diagonally. The last letter of each word starts the next word. You can use the same letter more than once. Start in the top left-hand corner.

с	р	а	е	т
п	о	н	т	е
о	т	а	с	н
р	е	с	р	а
т	с	т	о	п

1 **С** С п о р т
2 **Т** е а т р
3 **Р** у а н _ _ _ _ _
4 **Н** _ _
5 **Т** _ _ _
6 **С** _ _ _

6 You should now turn once more to your recorded material. There is a recording of a simple dialogue between a taxi driver and some people who have just called him to their flat. They are going to the Bolshoi Theatre. You will not understand all the dialogue. Look out for the words for:

hello	ZDRÁVSTVUYTE
please	POZHÁLUSTA
thank you	SPASÍBO
good	KHOROSHÓ
cheerio	DO SVIDÁNIYA

If you are working without a recording, practise pronouncing the words, making sure you get the stress in the right place.

Summary

You should now know how to say '*This is a/the . . . .*' '*No, this is not a . . . .*' You should also have learnt a few words of greeting and be able to recognise twelve of the 33 Russian letters and a number of Russian words, many of which are like English ones. Remember to get the stresses right when you pronounce them.

SHTO ÉTO?	ÉTO	KÁSSA TEÁTR METRÓ	(?)

	NYET, ÉTO NYE	KÁSSA TEÁTR METRÓ

KTO ÉTO?	ÉTO	PAPA MAMA

2
NOMER DVA

Where is... How is....?

Alphabet 2

Here are words containing the new letters for this unit. These words are recorded on your disc/cassette.

1	вода́ ☐	8	коммуни́зм ☐	15	да́та ☐
2	во́дка ☐	9	Ле́нин ☐	16	квас ☐
3	лимона́д ☐	10●	Пра́вда ☐	17●	апте́ка ☐
4	литр ☐	11●	Крокоди́л ☐	18●	мир ☐
5	кило́ ☐	12●	Кавка́з ☐	19	кио́ск ☐
6	киломе́тр ☐	13	зоопа́рк ☐	20	Толсто́й ☐
7	университе́т ☐	14●	дом ☐	21	Сове́тский, ☐

● **Пра́вда**, as well as meaning 'truth', is the name of the main Russian daily newspaper.

● **Крокоди́л** is often referred to as the Russian 'Punch'. It is a weekly satirical magazine containing a large number of cartoons.

● **Кавка́з**, *the Caucasus* is a range of mountains dividing Russia from the republic of Georgia.

The highest mountain in the range is Elbrus at 5633 m, the fifth highest mountain in the USSR and the highest point in Europe. The highest mountains in the USSR are in the Pamir (**Пами́р**) and Tyan' Shan' ranges and rise to a height of 7495 m.

Letters you know New letters	КОМЕТА СПРИНВ ЗДЛУЙ

- **дом** literally means 'house', but more often than not refers to a large block or an apartment building. When addressing a letter, it is abbreviated to д. This is usually followed by the number of the flat **кварти́ра** (**кв.**) and the name of the person for whom the communication is intended. *Fuller instructions on addressing letters occur in Unit 19.*

- **апте́ка** is a chemist's. Compare the English 'apothecary'.

- **мир** means both 'peace' and 'world'. There is a popular slogan ми́ру — мир, which appears on placards and on buildings. It means 'Peace to the World'.

1 ◌ As in Unit one, on the first reading there is a gap for you to repeat the word. On the second reading there is a gap after you hear the **но́мер** — *number* for you to read the word, then the correct version for you to check your reading. Use the boxes to record your score. If you feel satisfied with your reading, put a tick. If not, put a cross and repeat your attempt. Remember the stresses. All of the letters have sounds similar to English sounds. **й** (short '**и**') is pronounced like the *y* in *boy*.

2 ◌ Now we shall mix up the words. *If you are working without recorded material, you should proceed straight to exercise 3 (below).* You will hear a selection of them spoken in a different order. Look down the list and find the word that has just been read. Place the number of the word in the appropriate box below. For example, if you hear **но́мер оди́н** (NÓMER ODÍN) *number one* **КИЛОМЕ́ТР** you find **КИЛОМЕ́ТР** in the list and place 6 in the box next to number one. There are ten examples in the exercise.

1 ☐ 2 ☐ 3 ☐ 4 ☐ 5 ☐ 6 ☐ 7 ☐ 8 ☐ 9 ☐ 10 ☐

3 ◖ Here are some of the words above written in the Latin alphabet. Identify them by their original numbers, using the boxes provided. Put in the stresses.

1 LIMONAD ☐ 2 KILO ☐ 3 LENIN ☐ 4 PRAVDA ☐
5 KROKODIL ☐ 6 KAVKAZ ☐ 7 ZOOPARK ☐ 8 VODKA ☐
9 VODA ☐ 10 KILOMETR ☐

Вода́ (VODÁ) means *water*. GAZIRÓVANNAYA VODÁ — *fizzy water* is popular and costs 2 kopeks from a street machine. The Russians drink a good deal of **минера́льная вода́** (MINERÁL′NAYA VODÁ) *mineral water*. Some of them also drink **во́дка** (VODKA). The two words **вода́** and **во́дка** are obviously related, and come from the same root. This kind of relationship between words is very common in Russian and you should look out for it. It is often possible to split

14

See Grammar notes
(Word building) page 163

words up and, if you know what the different parts mean, to make a guess at the meaning of the whole word. We shall point this out from time to time in later units.

Other drinks commonly found in the USSR are **лимона́д, пи́во** *beer* and **квас** KVAS; the latter is normally served from a tank in the street. It is made from fermented black bread, and the alcohol content is very low.

* *See Grammar notes*
(Genders) page 154

You will have noticed that words have different endings.

— There are words which have 'no ending'*, like **орке́стр, стол** *table* and **пиани́ст**. These words are always referred to by **он** *he, it*.

— Words which end in **-a** are usually referred to by **она́** *she, it*. There are exceptions, e.g. **па́па**.

— Words ending in **-o** are usually referred to by **оно́** *it*.

— Plural words — **они́** *they*.

Grammar notes
(Locative) page 155

Endings can also change according to the *function* of a word in a sentence. For example, if you see the word **в** (*in, at*) or **на** (*on, at*), it is likely that the ending of the following word will be **-e**, e.g. **в теа́тре, на Кавка́зе**. Some words, especially some foreign ones, do not change at all, e.g. **такси́, метро́, кино́** (cinema).

4 📖 Look at the picture below and see how many things you can recognise in Russian. The question each time is

where is...? GDE...?

The answer is Вот он/а/о — there it is. You have to join the arrow to the correct object in the picture.

(GDE) **орке́стр?**	**Вот он** →
(GDE) **па́па?**	**Вот он** →
(GDE) **ма́ма?**	**Вот она́** →
(GDE) **пиани́ст?**	**Вот он** →
(GDE) **стол?**	**Вот он** →
(GDE) **во́дка?**	**Вот она́** →
(GDE) **вода́?**	**Вот она́** →
(GDE) **вино́?**	**Вот оно́** →
(GDE) **пи́во?**	**Вот оно́** →

5 📼 On your recording is a series of questions asking you where objects are. You have to supply the answers вот... with either он, онá or онó. A space is provided on the recording for your answer and then the correct answer is given. The boxes below are for you to tick your answers, if you are satisfied with your response. If not, try again.

☐　☐　☐　☐　☐　☐　☐　☐　☐　☐　☐

The word for How? is Как? Here are some questions using как and possible answers to them.

Question	*Answer*
Как вас зовýт?	**Вйктор.**
What is your name?	
(*lit. how do they call you?*)	
Как делá?	KHOROSHÓ, SPASÍBO
How are things?	NICHEVÓ.
	PLÓKHO.
Как дóма?	
How are things at home?	
Как мáма?	
How's your Mum?	

Как does not have to be part of a question. It may also be used as an exclamation, as follows.

Как PRIYÁTNO ZDES′!   *How pleasant it is here!*
Как ZDES′ KHOROSHÓ!   *How good it is here!*

6 📼 On your recording you will hear another 'meeting' dialogue. Listen carefully for the expressions listed above. In addition you will hear **дóма** *at home*, ÓCHEN′ RÁD/A *Pleased to meet you!*, as well as some of the words you learned in the first unit.

7 📖 Here is another alphabet square, slightly larger than the last one and containing more words. The rules are the same as before. See how many words you can find, starting in the top left-hand corner. The last letter of a word starts the next word and letters may be used more than once. If you find you're at a 'dead-end', try a different route.

к	н	е	т	а	р
а	р	а	п	а	к
в	о	т	п	м	и
к	т	о	р	а	н
а	о	с	е	п	о
з	о	е	р	е	м

1 _ _ _ _ _ _
2 _ _ _ _ _ _
3 _ _ _ _
4 _ _ _ _ _
5 _ _ _ _ _ _
6 _ _ _ _
7 _ _ _ _ _ _
8 _ _ _ _ _

Summary

You are now more than half-way through the alphabet. You should also be able to ask where things are GDE...? and be able to answer **Вот**.... You know the words for *he, she, it* and *they*, and which kinds of words they take the place of. You should also know some of the ways Russians use the word **как**. The way that many Russian words change at the end (e.g. after **в** and **на**) is also mentioned, but don't worry too much about that. It is dealt with more fully later on.

GDE	TEÁTR KÁSSA METRÓ	?
VOT	ON ONÁ ONÓ	
KAK	VAS ZOVÚT DELÁ MÁMA	?

3
NOMER TRI

Finding your way around

Alphabet 3

We are introducing five new letters in this unit. x (kh) is pronounced like 'ch' in 'loch'. It is the first letter in the word KHOROSHÓ (good). The other letters are ю (yu), б (b), ф (f) and ь (soft sign). This 'softens' the letter before it, but doesn't have a sound of its own. Listen carefully and see if you can hear what happens when -ь occurs.

⌫ Look at the words below and turn to your recorded material. You will hear each word spoken for you to imitate. The pattern is the same as for units one and two. This time we have also included a few words for revision purposes. You should be able to recognise the meaning of most of them. Use the box on the right of the word to indicate whether you are satisfied with your performance. If you are not, try again.

If you are working without recorded material turn to page 153 for approximate pronunciation.

1 футбо́л ☐	12 бульо́н ☐	22 узбе́к ☐
2 клуб ☐	13 ● Сове́тский	23 кли́мат ☐
3 сою́з ☐	Сою́з ☐	24 ● Дина́мо ☐
4 профсою́з ☐	14 кафе́ ☐	25 стадио́н ☐
5 фа́брика ☐	15 бюро́ ☐	26 ● Спарта́к ☐
6 вход ☐	16 фо́то ☐	27 ● Торпе́до ☐
7 костю́м ☐	17 ● Кремль ☐	28 ● Локомоти́в ☐
8 ● ВДНХ ☐	18 фильм ☐	29 ● ремо́нт ☐
9 меню́ ☐	19 ю́мор ☐	30 ● администра́тор ☐
10 перехо́д ☐	20 авто́бус ☐	31 ● хокке́й ☐
11 телефо́н ☐	21 буфе́т ☐	32 ● кино́ ☐

● **ВДНХ** are the initial letters of the permanent economic exhibition in Moscow, where each of the fifteen republics of the USSR exhibits its economic achievements.

● **Кремль**: the Kremlin. The word means *fortress* and is the seat of the Soviet government, as well as being the site of many beautiful cathedrals.

Letters you know New letters	КОМЕТА СПРИНВ ЗДЛУЙ ХЮБФЬ

● Russians are very keen on football. There are three main football grounds in Moscow: **Стадио́н Дина́мо**, **Стадио́н и́мени** *in the name of* **Ле́нина** and **Стадио́н Торпе́до**. Matches usually take place in the evenings, and grounds tend to be used by more than one team. Some teams may be associated with trades or professions, e.g. **Локомоти́в** is the team for railway workers.

● Another sport which has mass appeal in the Soviet Union is *ice-hockey* хоккéй. **Динáмо**, **Спартáк** and **Торпéдо** all have teams in the first division of the hockey league. They are not merely football clubs, but have many sports under their auspices. Other winter sports which are very popular are **катáние на конькáх** *skating* and **катáние на лыжах** *skiing*. During winter months many Russians go cross-country skiing in the outskirts of Moscow and other cities. Equipment can be hired very cheaply from ski-centres.

● **ремóнт** is a borrowed word from French and means repair. **На ремóнте** outside a shop or other public building means that it is closed for repairs.

● **администрáтор** is the *manager* of a hotel, restaurant or other large institution. *See also page 72.*

- **Кино́** *Cinema* going is extremely popular in the Soviet Union, and Soviet cinema is renowned throughout the world. The films of Eisenstein are considered among the best of early creative film-making, as are those of Pudovkin, Dovzhenko, Vertov and others.

NB *If you are working without recorded material turn to page 153 for approximate pronunciation.*

Most of the words listed above will be easily recognised from the English. Those which may not, include **Сою́з** SOYÚZ — '*Union*' as in **Сове́тский Сою́з** and СССР. **Профсою́з** PROFSOYÚZ — *trade union*. Notice that this last word has two parts and that the first part PROF- can easily be guessed from the English. Another two-part word is **вход**. The **в-** at the beginning means *in* or *en-*, and the second part has to do with going. The word means *entrance*. The entrance to the Metro is **вход в метро́** and '*let's go to the restaurant*' is 'POYDYÓM V RESTORÁN', with **в** here meaning *into*; similarly **вход в парк, вход в рестора́н**, etc. Notice that in these cases the end of the word stays the same. This is because there is movement involved (*compare page 15*).

Another word which can be split into two parts is **перехо́д**. As you know from -**хо́д**, the word has something to do with going. The first part means 'across' and **перехо́д** means 'crossing'. It is also used in the Metro to indicate crossing from one line to another.

Бюро́ (office) and **бульо́н** (clear soup) are examples of other words borrowed from French. **Фа́брика** should be obvious, the English word 'fabricate' is a clue to the meaning, i.e. 'factory'.

1 ⌧ Back to the sound recording. You will hear some of the words in the list above in a different order. As you hear each word spoken, look down the list and find it. Place its number in the appropriate box below. If you hear NÓMER ODÍN, number one **перехо́д**, you place number ten in the first box, etc. There are ten examples.

1 ☐ 2 ☐ 3 ☐ 4 ☐ 5 ☐ 6 ☐ 7 ☐ 8 ☐ 9 ☐ 10 ☐

📖 Here are some of the same words written in the Latin alphabet. See if you can recognise them from the list above. Use the boxes to check your answers.

1 AVTOBUS ☐	4 BUL'ON ☐	7 UZBEK ☐	10 TORPEDO ☐
2 PEREKHOD ☐	5 TELEFON ☐	8 BYURO ☐	
3 STADION ☐	6 KHOKKEY ☐	9 YUMOR ☐	

2 📖 In the last unit the question GDE? was asked, and the answer was он/она́/оно́/ там or вот он/она́, etc. Of course replies may be much more complex than this, especially if you ask the way on the street. Knowing what to expect is important, and helps you to pick out the key bits of the answer. Look at the sign below. It is a direction sign in a park. Which are to the right, and which to the left?

Mark → for направо or ← for налево.

авто́бус ☐	кино́ ☐	ка́сса ☐	телефо́н ☐
туале́т ☐	кафе́ ☐	буфе́т ☐	рестора́н ☐

If you approach someone in the street to ask the way it is polite to first use the word **Извини́те** or **Прости́те** *excuse me*.

3 🔊 Now listen to the recording. People are being asked where things are and are giving directions. Sometimes there will be one direction indicated, sometimes two, and sometimes three or four. If the first direction is to the right, place an arrow pointing to the right. If to the left, an arrow pointing to the left. If the direction is straight on (PRYÁMO), put an arrow pointing straight upwards. Each time we shall also ask whether the place is far — **далеко́?** If the place is a long way, put a tick under **далеко́**. Don't expect to understand everything you hear. Pick out the key points.

					далеко́?
1	метро́				
2	кино́				
3	стадио́н				
4	рестора́н				
5	такси́				

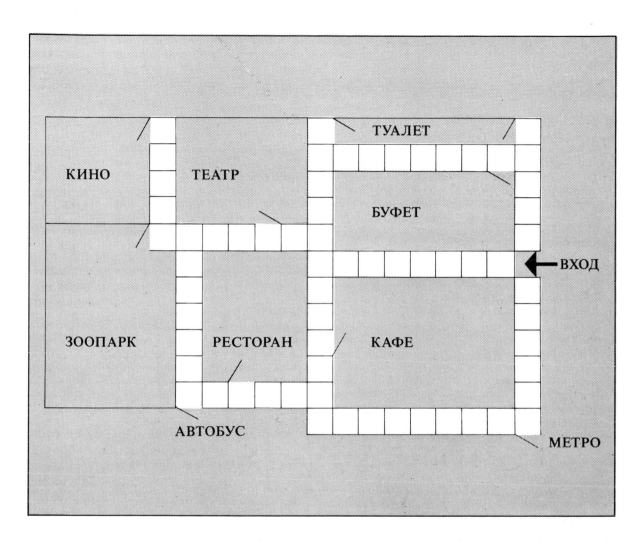

КИНО

ТЕАТР

ТУАЛЕТ

БУФЕТ

← ВХОД

ЗООПАРК

РЕСТОРАН

КАФЕ

АВТОБУС

МЕТРО

1   **В кафе́**
2   **В буфе́те**
3   **В зоопа́рке**
4   **В рестора́не**
5   **В туале́те**
6   **В теа́тре**
7   **В кино́**
8   **В авто́бусе**
9   **В метро́**

4 📖 Look at the maze above. You will be given directions. The numbers after the directions indicate the number of squares you have to move in that direction. You then have to say where you are in answer to the question GDE VY? (*where are you?*). Choose your response from those listed in the margin and place the number in the correct box. PRYAMO means *straight on*. Start at the same point — **Вход** — each time.

1	PRYAMO **8**	NALEVO **5**	NAPRAVO **3**	GDE VY?	☐
2	NALEVO **6**	NAPRAVO **8**	NAPRAVO **11**	GDE VY?	☐
3	NAPRAVO **4**	NALEVO **8**	NAPRAVO **1**	GDE VY?	☐
4	PRYAMO **8**	NAPRAVO **1**	NALEVO **6**	GDE VY?	☐
5	NALEVO **6**	NAPRAVO **8**	NAPRAVO **3**	GDE VY?	☐

23

5 Find your way. You are given the start and the destination. Find the shortest route marking the direction with arrows and putting in the number of squares moved, in the circle provided. The first one is done for you.

	Start	(напра́во = →	нале́во = ←	PRYÁMO = ↑)	Destination
1	Метро́	↑ ⑨	→①	←③	Рестора́н
2	Авто́бус	○	○	○	Кино́
3	Рестора́н	○	○	○	Зоопа́рк
4	Зоопа́рк	○	○	○ ○	Метро́
5	Кафе́	○	○	○	Теа́тр

6 Now back to the recording again. This time we are trying to find out whether a place is open, and, if not, when (KOGDÁ) it will be. The replies to listen for are OTKRÝT/A/O *open*, ZAKRÝT/A/O *shut*, VSEGDÁ *always*, SEYCHÁS *now*, ZÁVTRA *tomorrow*, SEVÓDNYA *today*. Write short answers in English.

Questions

1   Is the restaurant open? _____

2   When is the cinema open? _____

3   When is the cafe open? _____

4   Why is the buffet closed? _____

5   What do they have in the cafe? _____

7 Here is another alphabet game. This time make up as many Russian words as you can, using each letter once only. Initial letters are given in a different colour.

к е а ю ю р о о о о о о б б с з л ф ф ф у т т

1   Ф _ _ _ _ _

2   К _ _ _

3   Ф _ _ _

4   Б _ _ _

5   С _ _ _

8 Here are some jumbled words. See if you can decipher them. Use the boxes provided for your answers.

ЮМНЕ   1

НМДИОА   2

ЕХДПРОЕ   3

КРБАФИА   4

ИРЕЕНИУСВТТ   5

Summary

You should now know how to understand some more complex answers to the question 'GDE?'. You have also met some simple time expressions and some short adjectives, especially OTKRYT and ZAKRYT and have found out why some places are sometimes closed in the Soviet Union, e.g. **на ремóнте**.

IZVINÍTE, PROSTÍTE,	POZHÁLUSTA,	GDE	TELEFÓN KINÓ TUALÉT	?
NAPRÁVO NALÉVO PRYÁMO DALEKÓ	OTKRÝT/A/O ZAKRÝT/A/O VSEGDÁ/SEYCHÁS ZÁVTRA SEVÓDNYA			

4

NOMER CHETYRE

Asking permission

Alphabet 4

There are five new letters in this unit, and most of them are quite unlike any English letters. **Ё(ё)** is the exception, but even that is not pronounced anything like you might think it would be. The nearest English sound to it is YO with the 'O' pronounced short, like the sound in 'yacht'; **я** is pronounced YA, and on its own is the Russian word for 'I'. The others are **г** (G), **э** (E) as in 'extra' and **ы** (Y).

Here are the words which illustrate the alphabet for this unit. Listen to your recording and test your performance as before. Again, we have included a few words for revision purposes.

1	го́род ☐	11●	ГУМ ☐	20	О́льга ☐
2	телегра́мма ☐	12	экспре́сс ☐	21	май ☐
3	год ☐	13	эне́ргия ☐	22●	Неде́ля ☐
4	тури́сты ☐	14●	програ́мма ☐	23	ряд ☐
5	Аэрофло́т ☐	15●	пе́рвая	24	бланк ☐
6	самолёт ☐		програ́мма ☐	25●	Интури́ст ☐
7	экску́рсия ☐	16	вы́ход ☐	26	МГУ ☐
8 ●	Изве́стия ☐	17	выходи́ть ☐	27	ме́сто ☐
9 ●	газе́та ☐	18●	грибы́ ☐		
10●	Росси́я ☐	19●	о́рден ☐		

● **Изве́стия** is the second main newspaper in the Soviet Union. It is the organ of the COUNCIL OF PEOPLES' DEPUTIES. The word literally means '*News*'.

● The word for a *newspaper* is **газе́та** and can easily be recognised from the English 'Gazette'. **Литерату́рная газе́та** is the main literary newspaper. It contains articles on sociological problems, theatre, cinema, television, humour, foreign affairs, as well as on literature.

● **Росси́я** *Russia*, usually referred to as **РСФСР**, only one (albeit the largest) of the fifteen Republics of the USSR. It is also the name of the largest cinema and the largest hotel in Moscow.

Letters you know	КОМЕТА СПРИНВ ЗДЛУЙ ХЮБФЬ
New letters	ЭГЯЫЁ

● **ГУМ** is the state universal store in Red Square. Perhaps the most famous of Moscow stores, and certainly one of the longest established, being housed in a pre-revolutionary building. It is possible to buy most available goods there, but it is often very crowded, mostly with non-Muscovites who have come to Moscow on a shopping expedition. Mix the letters and you have **МГУ** — *Moscow State University*, which is situated on the Lenin Hills, the highest point in Moscow. The view from the Lenin Hills is a 'must' for most tourists and the University itself is a favourite Soviet showpiece, although it is difficult to get into it without a *pass* **пропуск**.

● **прогрáмма** can mean a theatre or football programme but is not normally used for a broadcast. It is used to indicate a radio channel or a TV channel, e.g. **Пéрвая прогрáмма** (lit. *First Programme*) is Moscow's equivalent of BBC 1.

● **грибы́** — Russians have a great liking for mushrooms of many kinds. There is a huge variety in the woods and forests around Moscow, and regular expeditions are organised to collect them. The mushrooms are then salted, dried, bottled, boiled, fried or stewed. Perhaps the best place to enjoy them is in a Russian home, if you are lucky enough to be invited.

- **о́рден** is a decoration or Order, not necessarily of a military nature. The highest award is **О́рден Ле́нина** — the *Order of Lenin*, but there are many more, including the Order of the Red Banner, the Order of the Patriotic War, the Order of the Red Banner of Labour, the Order of the Red Star, etc. Look out for them on people's lapels. You never know just who you may be standing next to!

- **Неде́ля** '*The Week*' is the weekly supplement of **Изве́стия**.

- **Интури́ст** is the state foreign tourist agency. It handles most of the travel arrangements for foreigners, both internally and at an international level, and deals mainly in 'hard' currency. Most arrangements (theatre tickets, meals, etc.) can be made by **Интури́ст**, but you might find it more fun to try and make some of your own arrangements. You should be in a position to do this when you have completed the course!

Most of the other words in the list you will easily recognise. Those that you may not are **го́род** — town, city. Notice that **Ленингра́д** has **-град** at the end, which means the same as **го́род**. Another word beginning with **г** is **год** meaning *year*. It is usually abbreviated to **г.**, so that you will see **1980г.** or **в 1980г. Аэрофло́т**, another two-part word, is the Soviet airline. The second part of the word, **-флот**, is the Russian word for *fleet*. **Самолёт** is an *aeroplane*.

In the last unit you came across the word **вход** meaning *entrance*. You will notice a similar word above, **вы́ход**, which means exactly the opposite. The first part of the word **вы-** usually indicates *out of*. Another word related to it is **выходи́ть** *to come out*. To enter is **входи́ть** as you might expect. Most words ending with **-ать** or **-ить** mean '*to do*' something.

Theatre tickets **биле́ты** have three important pieces of information on them, the date and time of the performance, the part of the theatre (e.g. **балко́н**, **парте́р**), *the row* **ряд** (RYAD) and the *seat number* **ме́сто**.

See Grammar notes (Verbs) page 160

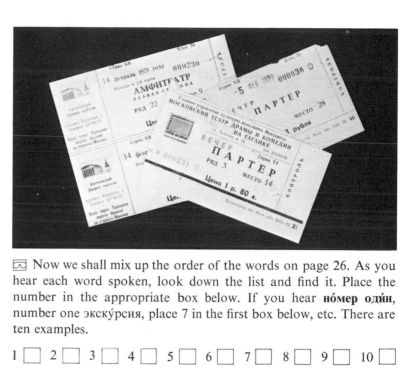

⌐ Now we shall mix up the order of the words on page 26. As you hear each word spoken, look down the list and find it. Place the number in the appropriate box below. If you hear **нóмер одúн**, number one экскýрсия, place 7 in the first box below, etc. There are ten examples.

1 ☐ 2 ☐ 3 ☐ 4 ☐ 5 ☐ 6 ☐ 7 ☐ 8 ☐ 9 ☐ 10 ☐

Here are some of the words written in the English (Latin) alphabet. See if you can recognise them from the list above. Use the boxes to check your answers. Put in the stresses.

1	GRIBY ☐	2	IZVESTIYA ☐	3	VYKHOD ☐
4	RYAD ☐	5	VYKHODIT′ ☐	6	ROSSIYA ☐
7	TELEGRAMMA ☐	8	SAMOLYOT ☐	9	ENERGIYA ☐
10	AEROFLOT ☐				

It is important for the visitor to the USSR to know what is allowed and what is not allowed in certain places. If you are unsure about whether something is permitted, you should use the word MÓZHNO? This is sometimes followed or preceded by the word that indicates what is permitted, e.g. **курить** MÓZHNO or MÓZHNO **курить**, it is permitted to smoke. The order of words in Russian is less strict than in English.

1 📖 Here are examples of notices that you might see around you in the Soviet Union forbidding things. See if you can guess what they mean. *Answers on page 166.*

не курить!	_____
вхо́да нет	_____
не фотографи́ровать!	_____
нет вы́хода	_____
здесь не ку́рят!	_____
перехо́да нет!	_____
по газо́нам не ходи́ть!	_____

One of the features of the Soviet Union is that smoking tends to be forbidden in many more places than in the West. Many buffets, cafes and other eating places have *No smoking* signs (**не кури́ть!**).

You may use the word MÓZHNO? as a general way of asking permission to do something without using all the words you intend to express, e.g.

бланк MÓZHNO? — *May I have a form?* (i.e. *for a telegram*)
газе́ту MÓZHNO? — *May I read your* (*the*) *newspaper?*

You will notice the **-у** on the end of **газе́ту**; **бланк** does not change.

30

See Grammar notes
(Cases) page 154

Not all words change in the same way, e.g. **Ива́на** MÓZHNO? means *Could you call Ivan to the telephone?* (i.e. *Is it possible to speak to him?*); **Ни́ну** MÓZHNO? *Can I speak to Nina?*. As you see, Russian can be very economical in the number of words used to express an idea. In reply to the question 'MOZHNO?' you may hear **нельзя́** *it's not allowed.*

2 ▬ Listen to the recording. You will hear a telephone conversation. A man is trying to make a date with a girl, Ol'ga. Listen to the conversation and see if you can answer the questions in English or Russian.

1 Who does the man speak to first?
2 Does she know him?
3 What is the man's name?
4 What does he want Ol'ga to do?
5 What is her reply?
6 When do they intend to go?

See Grammar notes
(Nouns) page 155

You may have noticed that some of the words in this unit end in -ы or -и (грибы́, тури́сты). You have already come across они́ (Unit 2). These letters very often mark a plural, just as -s does in English. Грибы́, for example, means 'mushrooms' and тури́сты 'tourists'. You can easily work out from this that тури́ст is one tourist and гриб is one mushroom. Words ending in -a also have -ы or -и in the plural, e.g. телегра́мма — телегра́ммы (telegrams), фа́брика — фа́брики. Sometimes, with 'borrowed' or 'imported' words, the result looks strange. Бу́тсы means 'football boots' and the singular is бу́тс 'a football boot'!

3 ◧ Here, in a jumbled form, are some of the words introduced in this lesson. See if you can work them out. Use the boxes provided. There is a hidden word in one of the vertical columns. Print it in the space provided.

1   **ырбиг**

2   **гмраомарп**

3   **нгяэире**

4   **торфоалэ**

5   **днрое**

Hidden word

31

4 📖 1 азгтае

2 нрутсиит

3 сскэрепс

4 исрясо

5 кярскиэус

6 ятвзисие

Hidden word

5 📖 Pick out the matching symbols and form words with the letters inside them. You are given the first letter in each word to help you.

1 **С** _ _ _ _ _ _

2 **Б** _ _ _ _ _

3 **П** _ _ _ _ _ _

4 **В** _ _ _ _ _

5 **Н** _ _ _ _ _ _

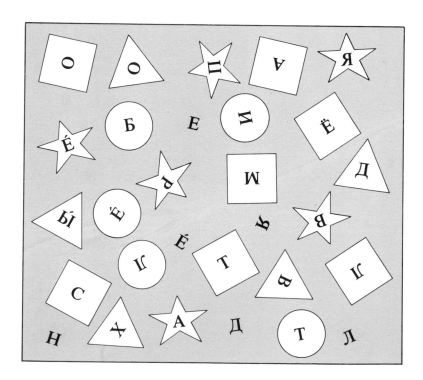

32

Summary

You now know how to ask permission to do something MÓZHNO___?
and have learned to understand a few prohibitions. You have come
across verbs (-ить, -ать words) and plurals ending in -ы and -и.

MÓZHNO	KURÍT´ FOTOGRAFÍROVAT´	?
BLANK GAZÉTU NÍNU	MÓZHNO	?

TURÍST	→	TURÍSTY
GRIB	→	GRIBÝ
TELEGRÁMMA	→	TELEGRÁMMY
FÁBRIKA	→	FÁBRIKI

5

Revision

Alphabet 5

The new letters in this unit are all quite unlike any English letters. **Ш**, for example, derives from the Hebrew as does **Ц**. All of the sounds they represent are rendered in English by more than one letter, and the English versions of them look very complex. You have already seen MOZHNO. The Russian version has one letter less **можно**. The word for *good*, KHOROSHO, has two letters less **хорошо**. **Щ** looks even more complicated in English: SHCH. Thus the Russian **Хрущёв** would be written in English KHRUSHCHOV. The reason why it sometimes appears as *Khrushchev* is because the English is taken from the printed version of Russian newspapers, where the two dots over the letter 'e' are not always used. **Ч** (CH) should not be confused with **У** (U).

The Russian for *tea* is **чай** (CHAI)*. **Чайко́вский** (CHAIKOVSKY) and **Чéхов** (CHEKHOV), for reasons we shall not go into here, are sometimes written with 'T' at the beginning in English. French equivalents look quite different (a French version of **Хрущёв**, for example, is *Khroutschiouw*, i.e. thirteen letters to render the Russian six, and the French version of **Пу́шкин** (*Pushkin*) is Pouchkine, i.e. nine letters instead of the Russian six). Other slavonic languages, many of which have similar sounds to Russian, also have different ways of writing these sounds. Polish, for example, has sz for **ш**, cz for **ч** and ż for **ж**. **Ц** as in **царь** is another common letter in this group. The group, as you will have noticed, consists of hissing sounds (sibilants) and **ъ** (hard sign), which only occurs in the middle of words and which does not have a sound of its own. Before the alpha-

---

* Tea used to be served from a samovar (самовар) which is a device for boiling water and keeping it hot. The tea is brewed in the normal way (in a teapot) and then diluted with water from the samovar. Samovars can still be bought in the Soviet Union, but they are the exception rather than the rule in the average Russian household. They can sometimes be seen in use in canteens and cafés, but, again, not universally.

Letters you know
New letters

КОМЕТА СПРИНВ ЗДЛУЙ ХЮБФЬ ЭГЯЫЁ
ЖЧШЩЦЪ

bet was reformed in 1918 **ъ** used to occur on the end of many words, but at the reform it was abolished in this position. Other letters which were abolished in the interests of simplification and in order to help spread literacy to the masses were **ѳ**, **ѣ**, and **i**. You will see all of these letters on pre-revolutionary posters and in films depicting life before 1918.

Extract from The Bolshevik decree reforming the alphabet in 1918

СОБРАНIЕ УЗАКОНЕНIЙ и РАСПОРЯЖЕНIЙ
РАБОЧЕГО и КРЕСТЬЯНСКАГО ПРАВИТЕЛЬСТВА.

17 Октября 1918 г.   № 74.   ОТДЕЛ ПЕРВЫЙ.

Декрет Совета Народных Комиссаров.

804. О введении новой орфографiи.

В цѣлях облегченiя широким массам усвоенiя русской грамоты и освобожденiя школы от непроизводительнаго труда при изученiи правописанiя, Совѣт Народных Комиссаров постановляет:

I. Всѣ правительственныя изданiя, перiодическiя (газеты и журналы) и неперiодическiя (научные труды, сборники и т. п.), все документы и бумаги должны с 15-го октября 1918 г. печататься согласно при сем прилагаемому новому правописанiю

II. Во всѣх школах Республики:

1. Реформа правописанiя вводится постепенно, начиная с младшей группы 1-й ступени единой школы.

2. При проведенiи реформы не допускается принудительное переучиванiе тѣх, кто уже усвоил правила прежняго правописанiя.

3. Для всѣх учащихся и вновь поступающих остаются в силѣ лишь тѣ требованiя правописанiя, которыя являются общими для прежняго и для новаго правописанiя, и ошибками считаются лишь нарушенiе этих правил.

Новыя правила правописанiя, разработанныя Народным Комиссарiатом Просвѣщенiя,

1. Исключить букву Ѣ. с послѣдовательной замѣной еѣ через Е.

2. Исключить букву Ѳ, с замѣной еѣ через Ф.

3. Исключить букву Ъ в концѣ слов и частей сложных слов, но сохранить ее в серединѣ слов, в значенiи отдѣлительнаго знака.

4. Исключить букву I, с замѣной ея через И.

5. Писать приставки из, воз, вз, раз, роз, низ, без, чрез, через—перед гласными и звонкими согласными с З, но замѣнять З буквой С перед глухими согласными, в том числѣ и перед С.

6. Писать в родительном падежѣ прилагательных. причастiй и мѣстоименiй ОГО. ЕГО—вмѣсто АГО, ЯГО.

7. Писать в именительном и винительном падежѣ женскаго и средняго рода множественнаго числа прилагательных, причастiй и мѣстоименiй—ЫЕ. ИЕ, вмѣсто ЫЯ, IЯ.

8. Писать ОНИ—вмѣсто ОНѢ в именительном падежѣ множественнаго числа женскаго рода.

9. Писать в женском родѣ—ОДНИ. ОДНИХ, ОДНИМИ вмѣсто ОДНѢ, ОДНѢХ, ОДНѢМИ.

10. Писать в родительном падежѣ единственнаго числа мѣстоименiя личнаго женскаго рода ЕЕ—вмѣсто ЕЯ.

Look at the order of the Russian alphabet and compare it with the English one.

а б в г д е ё ж з и й к л м н о п р с т у ф х ц ч ш щ ъ ы ь э ю я

As you see, there are 33 letters, three of which —

ъ (hard sign)   **ы** (y)   **ь** (soft sign)

do not occur at the beginning of a word*.

Notice also that the order of the alphabet is similar to English from и (i) to y (u) and that most of the 'exotic' letters occur towards the end. П is the most frequent initial letter with С fairly high on the list. The reason for this is that there are more 'prefixes' beginning with these letters (пере-, про-, по-, при-, с-/со-, etc.).

See Grammar notes (Prefixes) page 163

Here is a list of words containing the letters for this unit. Listen to your recording and check your performance on the second reading, as in previous units.

1	Чéхов ☐	12	Большóй	22	Хрущёв ☐
2 ●	Чáйка ☐		теáтр ☐	23 ●	щи ☐
3 ●	машúна ☐	13	москвúч ☐	24 ●	шáпка ☐
4	электрúчество ☐	14	этáж ☐	25 ●	жéнщина ☐
5 ●	электрификáция ☐	15	мóжно ☐	26 ●	цирк ☐
6	информáция ☐	16	хорошó ☐	27 ●	пóчта ☐
7 ●	бифштéкс ☐	17	шоссé ☐	28	ЦК ☐
8	шашлýк ☐	18	цветы́ ☐	29	цéнтр ☐
9	демонстрáция ☐	19 ●	куря́щий ☐	30	концéрт ☐
10	матч ☐	20 ●	некуря́щий ☐	31	бульвáр ☐
11 ●	Дворéц Съéздов ☐	21 ●	Крáсная		
			плóщадь ☐		

● **Чáйка** '*The Seagull*' is a play by **Чéхов**. It is also a make of Russian car (**машúна**) normally used to carry persons of high rank.

* й can sometimes occur at the beginning, but not in Russian words, e.g. Йорк (York) or Нью-Йорк (New York).

Other more common cars are **Во́лга** (VOLGA) and **Москви́ч** (MOSK-VICH), which means *Muscovite*. **Запоро́жец** (ZAPOROZHETS) is a very small car, not seen so frequently nowadays, especially since Fiat has set up a factory in **Тольятти**. One car designed by Fiat and manufactured in the USSR for export is the *Lada* (**Ла́да**), or as it is known in the USSR **Жигули́**.

● The meaning of **электрифика́ция** should be obvious. The ending **-ция** corresponds to the English -tion. Similar examples are: **информа́ция, конститу́ция, демонстра́ция**, etc. Note also that **-ство** in **электри́чество** corresponds to the English -ity.

● **Бифште́ксы** are often like hamburgers. **Бифштекс натура́льный** is an ordinary steak. **Шашлыки́** (SHASHLYKI) are barbecued pieces of lamb on a spit, larger than kebabs, usually served with spring onions, and can be obtained in a **шашлы́чная**.

See Grammar notes
(Prepositions) page 155

● **Дворе́ц Съе́здов** is the Palace of Congresses, a large palace in the Kremlin built in the early 60's. As well as Communist Party congresses, many performances of opera and ballet take place there, and it is well worth a visit for the tourist in Moscow. In summer, in the close season of the Bol'shoi, performances by the Bol'shoi company are staged in this theatre. Other famous theatres in Moscow include MXAT (*The Moscow Arts Theatre*) where Stanislavsky's traditions are followed, and **Совреме́нник**, **Теа́тр на Тага́нке** and **Теа́тр на Ма́лой Бро́нной** which are considered by many the most progressive modern theatres.

● As we pointed out earlier, smoking tends to be forbidden in more places than in Britain. Another word you will see in this context is **куря́щий**. **Для куря́щих** appears on the sides of smoking compartments on trains. **Для некуря́щих**, as you may guess, means *for non-smokers*.

● **Кра́сная пло́щадь**, *Red Square*, was given its name long before the Revolution. **Кра́сный**, as well as meaning *red* used to have the meaning *beautiful*. Today the usual word for *beautiful* is **краси́вый**.

● A traditional Russian dish is **щи** *cabbage soup* which is made from a meat stock, as is **борщ** *beetroot soup*. The latter is often served with a spoonful of *sour cream* **смета́на**.

● **ша́пка**, a *hat* which may be made of fur, and may have ear-flaps to keep out the frost.

● **же́нщина** is *woman*. The sign outside the ladies' toilet will usually be a large **Ж**. Men's toilets are marked **М** (**мужчи́на** *man*).

- The *Moscow State Circus* (**цирк**) is one of the most famous in the world, and now operates in two buildings simultaneously. The new building is near the *University* (**МГУ**) and the old one in the centre of Moscow.
- **по́чта** is a *post office*. It is often possible to have parcels wrapped and tied up in the main post offices and to buy collections of *stamps* (**ма́рки**) in sets, usually in commemorative folders. *Postcards* (**откры́тки**) can also be bought there. Notice the similarity of the word to **откры́т-а** *open*.

If you know French, you will easily recognise **шоссе́** as chaussée — *highway*, **бульва́р** — *boulevard*, and **эта́ж** — *floor*.

Цветы́ means *flowers*. Russians are very fond of flowers, and they are sold in the street all the year round. Georgian flower sellers come from Tbilisi on most days of the week. They sell their flowers in Moscow, and then return to Georgia for fresh supplies.

There are many abbreviations in modern Russian. You have already met **МГУ, ГУМ, СССР**. **ЦК** is another example of this. It sometimes occurs with **КПСС** after it. The full version is as follows:

ЦЕНТРА́Льный КОМИТЕ́т КОММУНИСТи́ческой ПА́РТИи СОВЕ́Тского СОЮ́За.

The important parts have been put in capitals to help you guess the meaning.

⌇ . Now listen to your recording. We have recorded ten of the words from the list above in a different order. When you hear a word, find it on the list and write its number in the box provided below. There are ten examples.

1 ☐   2 ☐   3 ☐   4 ☐   5 ☐   6 ☐   7 ☐   8 ☐   9 ☐   10 ☐

Here are some of the words written in the Latin alphabet. See if you can recognise them from the list above. Use the boxes to check your answers. Put in the stresses.

1	TSVETY	☐	5	ETAZH	☐	8	KURYASHCHIY	☐
2	BIFSHTEKS	☐	6	SHCHI	☐	9	TSENTR	☐
3	SHOSSE	☐	7	ZHENSHCHINA	☐	10	SHASHLYK	☐
4	SHAPKA	☐						

1 ⌇ Now turn again to your recording. You will hear a conversation about what is going on at various places in Moscow. Each time the question **что идёт в** …? *What's on in . . . ?* is asked, the person who is about to answer the question looks at **Театра́льная Москва́** (a poster, giving details of what's on in the theatre) and then gives the reply.

You have to match the events and places using the lists below. Join up the words to form sentences and then check your answers on *page 167*. If you are working without a recording, make up your own answers.

во Дворце́ Съе́здов	идёт	фильм
в па́рке	идёт	о́пера
в университе́те	идёт	бале́т
в кино́	идёт	конце́рт
в Большо́м теа́тре	идёт	ле́кция

2 📖 Here are some jumbled words. This time the two hidden words may be vertical or diagonal and will answer the question что идёт в театре? Put the stress mark on the words, including the hidden ones.

1 оомнж

2 чптао

3 вхеоч

4 ёщхурв

5 жнаимуч

6 что идёт в теа́тре?

3 📖

1 кйача

2 сеошс

3 фцмярииноа

4 ртнце

5 щанижен

6 ршхооо

7 чтма

8 что идёт в теа́тре?

Revision

a 📼 Here is a test for revision purposes. It is assumed that you now know the alphabet and that if you do not, you will go over the alphabet sections again before attempting the test.

		Answer
Это рестора́н.	Вот Ви́ктор.	**Он в рестора́не**
э́то теа́тр	вот пиани́ст	_____
э́то парк	вот ма́ма	_____
э́то парк	вот ма́ма и па́па	_____
э́то Ленингра́д	вот кино́	_____
э́то Москва́	вот Кра́сная пло́щадь	_____

41

э́то зоопа́рк	вот жира́ф	_____
э́то апте́ка	вот Ве́ра	_____
э́то рестора́н	вот орке́стр	_____
э́то кварти́ра	вот самова́р	_____
э́то автома́т	вот лимона́д	_____

b Choose the correct alternative. The first one is done for you.

Москва́ в ────── Сове́тском Сою́зе
Áнглии
Аме́рике

Кра́сная пло́щадь
в Ленингра́де
в це́нтре Москвы́
на стадио́не

Это вы́ход. Здесь нельзя́
переходи́ть
выходи́ть
входи́ть

Это вход. Здесь мо́жно
входи́ть
выходи́ть
чита́ть

Это вы́ход. Здесь нет
вхо́да
вы́хода
перехо́да

На стадио́не сейча́с идёт
конце́рт
матч
крокоди́л

c Here is a drawing with some signs and objects on it. You have to match the Russian words with the signs and objects by placing the appropriate letter in the box provided next to the Russian.

42

автобусы ☐

мужчины ☐

касса ☐

женщины ☐

выход ☐

метро ☐

не курить ☐

такси ☐

девушка ☐

телефон-автомат ☐

Summary

The only new item you have learned in this unit is **идёт** (lit. *is going* or *is going on*.) The alphabet is now complete, and you will not see any more items 'transliterated'.

43

6

Buying things

This unit is about the language you need in order to buy things. If you want to ask whether something is available, you can do it by using the expression **'у вас есть...?'** *have you got...?* or, simply, **'есть...?'** *is there any...?*. In a restaurant or shop you might ask — **девушка, у вас есть пиво?** The answer to this might be — **да, есть** or **нет, пива нет.** If the answer is positive, the girl might then ask — **сколько вам...?** *'how many do you want?'* (i.e. bottles or glasses). You would then reply — **дайте мне...** *'give me...'*. You will then want to know *how much* — **сколько стоит?** or just **сколько?**

See Grammar notes (Genitive) page 155

This all involves you in the use of numbers. If you have access to the recorded material, you will already have heard Russian numerals repeated on many occasions. Counting 1–10 in Russian is fairly simple. Russians take fitness very seriously and each morning on the radio there are *morning exercises* (**утренняя зарядка**) to music with the count of **раз, два, три, четыре** (1–4). In this sort of count **раз** *once* takes the place of **один** *one*. **Три** *three* is obviously very like the English and **два** begins with the same Russian letter as the English 'double', 'duet', 'duo'.

See Grammar notes (Numerals) page 162

The rest of the numbers from 5–10 are:

пять 5   **шесть** 6   **семь** 7   **восемь** 8   **девять** 9   **десять** 10

The one that most English people have trouble with is **де́вять**. **Де́сять** can be easily remembered from DECimal.

Де́вушка is a way of addressing a woman of any age, if she is a waitress or shop assistant. A *small girl* would be addressed as **де́вочка**. *Women* (**же́нщины**) can be found in unexpected occupations in the Soviet Union, e.g. *engineers* **инжене́ры**, builders, etc., and the majority of doctors and teachers are women. To some extent this is due to the fact that large numbers of men were lost in the war, and in certain age groups there is a distinct shortage of males.

The exchanges below might take place in a **буфе́т** (*buffet*).

Customer	Waitress
Де́вушка, у вас есть пи́во?	Нет, пи́ва нет.
	Да, есть.
Что у вас есть?	Конья́к.
	Вино́.
	Шампа́нское.
	Чай.
	Ко́фе.
Ско́лько сто́ит шампа́нское?	Пять рубле́й.
	Четы́ре рубля́.
Да́йте, пожа́луйста, оди́н чай и оди́н конья́к.	Хорошо́.
	Вот вам чай и конья́к.
	Вот ва́ше шампа́нское.
Ско́лько?	Рубль де́сять.
	Плати́те, пожа́луйста, в ка́ссу.
Хорошо́.	

The usual way to buy things in the Soviet Union is to find out how much you have to pay for a purchase, then obtain a receipt (**чек**) from the **ка́сса**, and present the receipt to obtain your goods.

раз   два   три   четы́ре

1 👓 The first exercise is repetition with a difference. You will hear a customer asking for something and then finding out how much it is. Repeat the request and answer, and then write down the amount it costs in the box provided under the picture below.

р. коп.	р. коп.	р. коп.
р. коп.	**р. коп.**	**р. коп.**

2 👓 Now listen to your recording again. You will hear a conversation between a hotel guest and a girl at the *Service Bureau* (**Бюро́ обслу́живания**). There is one of these in most hotels, and the women there are sometimes very helpful in providing advice and information on booking cars, restaurants, theatre tickets and flights, as well as arranging tourist excursions. They often speak English but will, no doubt, be pleased if you can speak to them in Russian.

Answer the following questions in English or Russian:

1 What does the guest want? _____

2 Why can't he get it? _____

3 What does he suggest as an alternative? _____

4 What is the reply? _____

5 How many tickets does he finally order? _____

6 What does he have to pay? _____

Written Russian is not exactly the same as printed Russian, but you will recognise most of the letters without a great deal of trouble. One letter which is not written as it is printed is т written *m* as in *фото* **фото** or *спутник* **спутник**. Notice that п in *спутник* is written exactly like an English n. Д is written *g* or *∂* e.g. *дом* **дом**.

Сегодня
МЕЖДУНАРОДНЫЙ ДЕНЬ МУЗЕЕВ
ВХОД В ГОСУДАРСТВЕННЫЙ

Russian currency has the following denominations: paper money comes in 1, 3, 5, 10, 25, 50 and 100 ruble notes. Small change **ме́лочь** comes in 1, 2, 3, 5, 10, 15, 20 and 50 kopek pieces (**моне́ты**). Ruble coins usually commemorate some historical event and they tend to become collectors' pieces.

It is a good idea to keep a supply of small change. A telephone call from an **автома́т** *call box* costs **две копе́йки** 2 *kopeks* and the Метро́ costs **пять копе́ек** 5 *kopeks* any distance. If you have the wrong money in the Метро́, look for an **автома́т** *change machine*. Tickets are never used in the **Метро́**, and access is gained by putting a coin in an automatic barrier. Vending machines also accept **моне́ты** *coins* and all forms of public transport operate without a conductor. **Авто́бусы** also cost **пять копе́ек**, and **троллéйбусы — четы́ре копе́йки**. **Трамва́й** costs **три копе́йки**, any distance. Because of the inconvenience of handling change, Russians often buy a season ticket **проездно́й биле́т** or **еди́ный биле́т**, which allows them to travel on any form of public transport for a *month* **на ме́сяц**; or they may buy *a book of tickets* **тало́ны**. These are obtainable from the driver.

3 🔊 Now turn once more to your recording. A man is trying to make a telephone call from an **автома́т**. He gets the wrong number at the first attempt and has to ask a passer-by for some more change. Listen for — **Алло́: слу́шаю вас** (that's the first thing you hear when you get through), **вы не туда́ попа́ли,** or **не тот но́мер:** *wrong number,* **перезвони́те:** *try again.*

КРОССВÓРД

Clues Across

1   семь, вóсемь _____
4   Central Committee
6   No!
7   I
9   раз, два _____ четы́ре
11   Opposite of *НЕТ*
12   Swan Lake, for instance
14   In, into, in some places
15   A fur one to keep out the cold
18   Storey, floor
20   A telephone might be this, though
      not automatically...
22   Cabbage soup
23   He, it
24   A telephone has one, and so does
      a room in a hotel
26   Eating place
28   A very big store
29   Soviet Press Agency
31   Port on the Black Sea, famous for
      its steps*
32   Halt!
33   Every car has one
34   She

Clues Down

1   Young lady
2   The thing to say when you point
     at something
3   Three
5   The place to go when 26 across is
     закры́т
8   кинó or кафé or метрó can each
     be replaced by this but not by 34
     across
10   A kind of 'pop' music
13   This for peace
14   You
16   Марс, Юпи́тер for example*
17   Costs пять копéек
18   This
19   Moscow football club
21   Joke or anecdote*
25   Гóрод в Лáтвии*
27   English starts this place with a U
29   Не _____ нóмер!
30   Sometimes starts a meal*

Here is a Russian crossword. You have met almost all the words. The clues for the ones you have not met are marked with *. You should be able to guess them fairly easily. *Answers on p. 168.*

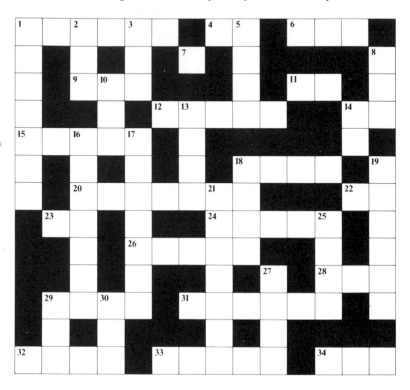

a   Complete the following referring to the crossword. Don't forget to change the endings in the second column. The first one is done for you.

1 down	дéвушка	в	31 across	Одéссе
15 across	_____	на	1 down	_____
12 across	_____	в	25 down	_____
33 across	_____	в	17 down	_____

b Find the clue, write the answer, and then print the number of the clue in Russian. The first one is done for you.

Central Committee	ЦК	но́мер четы́ре (4)
Раз, два _____ четы́ре		но́мер _____
I		но́мер _____
Young lady		но́мер _____
The thing to say when you point at something		но́мер _____
The place to go when 26 across is закры́т		но́мер _____
No!		но́мер _____
Three		но́мер _____
[Which numbers between 1–10 are missing?]		но́мер _____
		но́мер _____

Summary

You are now equipped to shop for anything that costs less than ten rubles or ten kopeks! Numerals occur throughout the rest of the course, and there is a check-list on *page 162*. The important grammatical item to notice is the way the endings of the words change after numbers, after ско́лько and after нет.

See Grammar notes (Genitive) page 155

у вас	есть	конья́к пи́во чай	?

ско́лько (сто́ит)	?

Who's who and how to address them

We have come across names ending in **-ский**, e.g. **Чайко́вский**. Mrs **Чайко́вский** would be called **Чайко́вская** and if you were talking about 'the Chaikovskies', you would use the form **Чайковские**. **Чайковский** is a surname, or family name, **фами́лия**. The normal way that Russians address one another is by using the word **това́рищ** *comrade*, but this, of course, often has political overtones, and a Russian would not normally use the word to a foreigner if he recognised him as such. **Друг** *friend* is a more likely alternative, or **колле́га** *colleague*. **Наш англи́йский колле́га** — notice the **-ий**. **Мой друг** '*my friend*' would mean that the person being referred to was a close friend. By **знако́мый (-ая, -ые)** *acquaintance*, i.e. a less close relationship is indicated. **Това́рищ** is used for males and females, but **граждани́н** *citizen* has a feminine form **гражда́нка**.

   If you are introduced to someone, the likely expression you will hear is '**Разреши́те предста́вить**' '*Allow me to present*' (formal) or '**Познако́мьтесь, пожа́луйста**' '*Please introduce yourselves*' (less formal). In a formal situation a Russian often gives his surname first and then follows it with his first name and patronymic (**и́мя и о́тчество**), e.g. **Петро́в, Бори́с Ива́нович**. The patronymic indicates that the man's father's first name is **Ива́н**. If you are introduced to Russians in a business or other formal situation, it's most polite to use the name and patronymic.

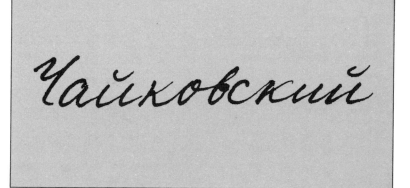

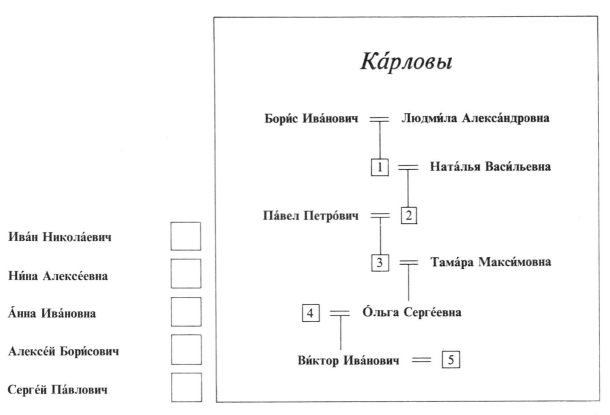

Ка́рловы

Бори́с Ива́нович = Людми́ла Алекса́ндровна

1 = Ната́лья Васи́льевна

Па́вел Петро́вич = 2

3 = Тама́ра Макси́мовна

4 = О́льга Серге́евна

Ви́ктор Ива́нович = 5

Ива́н Никола́евич

Ни́на Алексе́евна

А́нна Ива́новна

Алексе́й Бори́сович

Серге́й Па́влович

1 📖 Complete the Karlov family tree above. Look for the name of the father and match it with its patronymic from the list in the margin. Put the numbers in the boxes at the side of the name you select. Fathers and sons are on the left and mothers and daughters on the right. = means 'married to.'

If you are on name and patronymic terms with someone, you will normally use the form **вы** *you*. People who are on close terms with one another use **ты** '*thou*'. This has a parallel with many other European languages (compare French vous/tu, German Sie/du), but the distinction in English has, of course, long disappeared in standard speech. The transition from formal to informal is often a conscious one. **Мо́жно на ты?** or **Дава́йте на ты** (Let's use **ты** to each other). If you were talking to a very small child, you would expect to call him **ты** and the form is often used to indicate affection or familiarity. In certain circumstances it can indicate contempt for the person addressed.

If the relationship between individuals is a familiar one (they are on **ты** terms), the 'diminutive' form of the name is often used.

51

Notice that names of males often end in **-а** or **-я** in the diminutive form. Here are a few examples:–

Male	Female	Diminutive
Влади́мир		Воло́дя
Михаи́л		Ми́ша
Ю́рий		Ю́ра
Ива́н		Ва́ня
	О́льга	О́ля
	А́нна	А́ня
	Гали́на	Га́ля
	Ири́на	И́ра
	Ната́лья	Ната́ша
Алекса́ндр	Алекса́ндра	Са́ша
Евге́ний	Евге́ния	Же́ня

Besides using 'diminutive' forms which have a direct parallel in English (James = Jimmy, etc.), Russians very often use forms which have endearment built into them, and forms which indicate contempt. The endearment forms often end in **-ечка**, **-очка**, **-енька**, **-ушка**, or **-юшка**. Some names have more than one of these forms. **Ива́н** *John* is one of the most common Russian names and it has at least five 'endearment' forms (**Ваню́ша, Ва́нечка, Ваню́шечка, Ваню́шка,** and **Ива́нушка**) but only one 'contempt' form **Ва́нька**.

When addressing friends or children the formality of greetings also varies depending on the closeness of relationship. **Здра́вствуйте** becomes **Здра́вствуй** i.e. it loses the -**те** at the end. If you are asking someone familiar to say something the shorter form can be used, e.g. **скажи́те** becomes **скажи́**.

See Grammar notes (Imperatives) page 161

Look at the following pairs of sentences. The one on the left is formal, the one on the right informal. The forms are not necessarily totally parallel, but the ones on the right are more likely in an informal situation. The word **Приве́т** *greetings* is the usual informal way of saying 'hello'. **У нас, у вас, у меня́** are used, as you discovered in an earlier unit, to mean *we have, you have, I have*. They are also used in the sense of *in our place, in our country*, etc., e.g. **у нас до́ма, у нас в А́нглии; у нас в СССР**. Compare also the French 'chez'.

Formal	Informal
Здра́вствуйте, Ви́ктор Ива́нович. Как вы пожива́ете? Говори́т Ивано́в.	Здра́вствуй, Ви́тя. Как пожива́ешь? Это Бо́ря
А, Бори́с Миха́йлович! Ну, как дела́ у вас в Ки́еве?	Бо́ря! Как там у тебя́ в Ки́еве?
Мари́я Ива́новна, пойдёмте на ле́кцию.	Ма́ша, пойдём на ле́кцию.

2 Now turn to your recording. An older person is talking to a child. Listen for **как тебя́ зову́т?** (*What are you called? Lit. How do they call you?*). **Как вас зову́т?** is the formal way of asking *What are you called?*

Parallel forms are: **говоря́т, что**...*it is said that* (they say that)

See Grammar notes (они́) page 159   **игра́ют**...*is played* (they play)

as in **здесь игра́ют в футбо́л**...*football is played here.*

1	What is the child's name?
2	What is she playing with?
3	How old is the child?
4	What does her father work at?
5	How many postcards are there?

See Grammar notes (Adjectives) page 158

You have already met the forms **Сове́тский Сою́з, Большо́й теа́тр, Кра́сная пло́щадь, пе́рвая програ́мма, минера́льная вода́.** Notice how the endings above change. If you want to call an '-o' noun 'red', it becomes **кра́сное**, e.g. **кра́сное вино́** *red wine*; **-ы** or **-и** in **-ые, -ие**, as usual, signals a plural — **ру́сские** *Russians*, **краси́вые же́нщины** *beautiful women*.

53

3 📖 Look at the following and match them up to make sentences. Most of the words you will already know. The rest you can guess. Use one item from each of the three columns in each sentence. Do the obvious ones first. Join the words together with a line. The first one is done for you.

1	**О́льга Ко́рбут**	кра́сное	футболи́сты
2	**Ни́кон**	англи́йский	порт
3	**Де́вушка, у вас есть**	америка́нская	шампа́нское
4	**Джон-Поль II**	япо́нский	Па́па
5	**На столе́**	пе́рвый по́льский	газе́та
6	**Дина́мовцы**	сове́тский	фотоаппара́т
7	**Нью-Йорк Таймс**	украи́нский	вино́
8	**Бори́с**	сове́тское	до́ктор
9	**Оде́сса**	хоро́шие	го́род
10	**Манче́стер**	сове́тская	спортсме́нка

Many of the words in this unit are to do with nationalities — **ру́сский, англи́йский, америка́нский**, etc. Notice that the words normally begin with a small letter. Names of countries usually start with a large letter, e.g. **Сове́тский Сою́з**. Look at these examples.

Country	Nationality	Male	Female
Росси́я	ру́сский	ру́сский*	ру́сская
А́нглия	англи́йский	англича́нин	англича́нка
Аме́рика	америка́нский	америка́нец	америка́нка
Япо́ния	япо́нский	япо́нец	япо́нка
Украи́на	украи́нский	украи́нец	украи́нка
Гру́зия	грузи́нский	грузи́н	грузи́нка
Узбекиста́н	узбе́кский	узбе́к	узбе́чка
Кита́й	кита́йский	кита́ец	китая́нка
А́фрика	африка́нский	африка́нец	африка́нка

* Notice that all the words except ру́сский have a special word for the person.

4 Here is a map of the world. Connect the people to their place of origin.

рýсский ① англичáнин ② китáец ③ америкáнец ④ грузи́нка ⑤ африкáнец ⑥ япóнка ⑦ узбéк ⑧

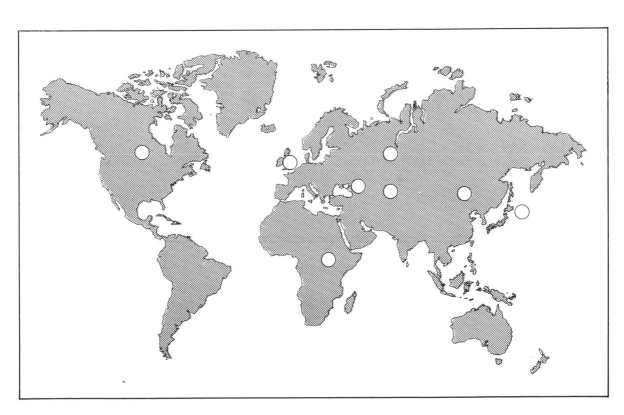

5 Decipher the illustrated written forms and print them underneath the illustrations.

Summary

You should have learned something about formality and informality in Russian; how to find out someone's name and greet them accordingly; and about the way adjectives change according to the nouns they go with. Remember that nationalities always start with a small letter, and the names of countries with a large one.

как	вас	зову́т	?
	тебя́		

меня́ зову́т	Бори́с
	Ни́на
	Ната́ша

мо́жно на ты?	:	здра́вствуйте → здра́вствуй
		скажи́те → скажи́
		пойдёмте → пойдём

у нас	до́ма
	в А́нглии
	в СССР

8

Likes and dislikes

There is the same distinction in Russian as in English between liking (мне нра́вится — I like, вам/тебе́ нра́вится — you like) and loving (я люблю́ — I love; вы лю́бите — you love). Look at the following examples:

Я люблю́ му́зыку	Мы лю́бим кино́
Я люблю́ теа́тр	Она́ мне нра́вится
Он лю́бит спорт	Вам нра́вится э́та програ́мма?
Она́ лю́бит те́ннис	Вам нра́вится матч?
Вы лю́бите футбо́л?	Москва́ мне нра́вится
	Тебе́ нра́вится э́тот фильм?

Я люблю́ etc. tends to refer to general 'liking' and **мне нра́вится** etc. to specific events or things. Degrees of liking are expressed in the following examples. Notice that if you want to say 'very much' you simply add the word **о́чень** (*very*) e.g. **Я о́чень люблю́ теа́тр** *I like the theatre very much.*

Вам нра́вится Москва́? Да, о́чень.

Я о́чень люблю́ Ло́ндон.

Вам нра́вится э́та де́вушка? Не о́чень.

You can also use both forms to say you like *doing* something, in which case the pattern looks like this:

Я люблю́ Мне нра́вится	игра́ть гуля́ть чита́ть танцева́ть смотре́ть телеви́зор	*to play* *to go walking* *to read* *to dance* *watching TV*

You have seen in earlier units how the endings of some words change (**ко́мната — в ко́мнате, в ко́мнату**, etc.). The endings of verbs ('doing' words) also change depending on who is performing the action. **Говоря́т, игра́ют, зову́т** (Unit 7) are all examples of this. 57

See Grammar notes (Verbs) page 160

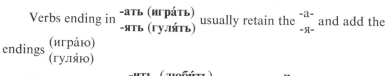

They are examples of the '**они**' *they* form. **Я** (I) is usually followed by the ending **-ю** or **-у** (**говорю́, люблю́, игра́ю, иду́**).

Verbs ending in **-ать (игра́ть)** / **-ять (гуля́ть)** usually retain the **-а-** / **-я-** and add the endings (**игра́ю**) / (**гуля́ю**)

Those ending in **-ить (люби́ть)** / **-еть (смотре́ть)** lose the **-и-** / **-е-** (e.g. **смотрю́**).

Люби́ть is a little unusual in that it adds an **-л-** (**люблю́**) but this happens only in the 'I' form. Look at the examples below, and notice how the endings change.

Он лю́бит футбо́л
Она лю́бит смотре́ть телеви́зор
Они́ лю́бят гуля́ть
Мы лю́бим хокке́й (we)
Вы лю́бите спорт?

Notice the word order in the last example, a question is unchanged. The question is asked by the tone of voice, as can happen in English.

1 Here is a matching exercise. Join the boxes together to form complete sentences.

Я	говоря́т по-ру́сски
Он	нра́вится танцева́ть
Вы	игра́ю в футбо́л
Они́	гуля́ете в па́рке
Он	смотрю́ телеви́зор
Я	лю́бит игра́ть на гита́ре
Мне	говори́т по-англи́йски

A very common word in Russian is **по** as in **по-ру́сски** *in Russian*. It also means, among other things, *along* (**по коридо́ру** — *along the corridor*) and the word following it has a changed ending. Sometimes the two words are joined together with a hyphen: по-мо́ему (in my

*See Grammar notes
(Prepositions) page 155*

opinion), по-вáшему (in your opinion), but more often the words are separate: по телевúзору (on television) or по Москвé (around Moscow). A two-part word which contains по as a 'prefix' is почемý? (why?) to which the answer is потомý что (because). Look at the following examples.

Question	Answer
Почемý ресторáн закрыт?	Потомý что идёт ремóнт.
Почемý вы гуляете в пáрке?	Потомý что там хорошó.
Почемý вы любите тéннис?	Потомý что я óчень хорошó игрáю.

2 ☐ Listen to your recording. Four people are talking about leisure and work. Their names are **Сáша**, **Вúктор**, **Áнна** and **Нúна**. Listen particularly for the following information:

1	What is Nina's occupation?
2	What does Anna like doing in the evenings?
3	What does Sasha do in his spare time?
4	Which TV programmes do they all like?
5	Which does Victor like?
6	Why doesn't Sasha's brother play football any more?

The twenty-four hour clock is widely used in the Soviet Union, especially on radio and television. To follow this you will need to know the numbers from 11 to 24. Here they are. First, the numbers from 11 to 20.

11	одúннадцать	16	шестнáдцать
12	двенáдцать	17	семнáдцать
13	тринáдцать	18	восемнáдцать
14	четырнадцать	19	девятнáдцать
15	пятнáдцать	20	двáдцать

If the words appear long at first, notice that the endings are all **-дцать** (a contraction of **де́сять** — *ten*) and that the numbers from 11 to 19 all have **-на́дцать** (i.e. 'on ten') at the end and that the beginnings of the words are very much like 1–9.

The numbers beyond twenty are:

21 два́дцать оди́н
22 два́дцать два
23 два́дцать три
24 два́дцать четы́ре etc.

3 Here are some times. Write them in numbers on the right.
Ско́лько вре́мени? *What time is it?*

1	Восемна́дцать часо́в два́дцать мину́т	
2	Два́дцать оди́н час пять мину́т	
3	Два́дцать два часа́ де́сять мину́т	
4	Девятна́дцать часо́в пятна́дцать мину́т	
5	Двена́дцать часо́в два́дцать две мину́ты	
6	Пятна́дцать часо́в два́дцать пять мину́т	
7	Семна́дцать часо́в три мину́ты	
8	Трина́дцать часо́в шестна́дцать мину́т	
9	Четы́рнадцать часо́в два́дцать де́вять мину́т	
10	Де́сять часо́в два́дцать мину́т	

4 There are eleven time zones in the Soviet Union. Look at the map on *page 64/5* and then try to answer the questions by filling in the blanks.

Кото́рый час? *What time is it?*

1 Когда́ в Москве́ 9 часо́в, в Ирку́тске _____ час ____

2 Когда́ в Москве́ 6 часо́в, во Владивосто́ке _____ час ____

3 Когда́ в Москве́ 12 часо́в, в Магада́не _____ час ____

4 Когда́ в Москве́ 4 часа́, в Ташке́нте _____ час ____

5 Когда́ в Москве́ 5 часо́в, в Баку́ _____ час ____

NOTE: 2 to 4, use **часа́** (also 22–24, 32–34 etc.)
From 5 upwards use **часо́в** (also 25–30, 35–40).

Moscow television has four channels each of which is referred to as Прогрáмма — Пéрвая Прогрáмма is the main channel and contains a wide variety of programmes. It starts at 8.00 a.m. and finishes about midnight. The main current affairs programme is 'Врéмя' (Time). This is usually shown twice a day, early in the morning and half-way through the evening. Most live popular programmes appear on this channel. Вторáя прогрáмма (channel 2) and Четвёртая прогрáмма (Channel 4) are mainly devoted to films of various kinds including concerts of classical music and documentaries. Трéтья прогрáмма (Channel 3) is an educational channel. School timetables are standard throughout the Soviet Union, so it is possible for educational television producers to pick out parts of the curriculum relevant to all schools and make programmes on them. If you look at the Russian weekly equivalent of the 'Radio Times' — Телевúдение—Рáдио, you might see the following programme description under Трéтья прогрáмма — 8.40, 9.40 Зоолóгия 7-ой класс.

Now look at the following TV programmes adapted from Вечéрняя Москвá, the main evening paper in Moscow, which is the place to look for entertainment. Нóвости (see нóвый (new), means 'News').

СЕГÓДНЯ   ПÉРВАЯ ПРОГРÁММА

18.00 — Нóвости.

18.15 — Вáльсы П. И. Чайкóвского — игрáет оркéстр Большóго теáтра.

18.25 — Концéрт Государственного академúческого заслýженного украúнского нарóдного хóра úмени Г. Верёвки.

19.10 — «Москвá и москвичú».

19.30 — Футбóл. Сбóрная СССР — сбóрная Грéции.

21.00 — «Врéмя». Информациóнная прогрáмма.

21.30 — Вéчер поэ́зии Ю. Дрýниной.

22.20 — Тирáж «Спортлотó». По окончáнии — нóвости.

5 ■ Now answer the following questions in English. If the programme description is complex, put down the essential points. Your answer should look like the entry in an English newspaper, but with the times based on the 24-hour clock. The first one is done for you.

1 Что идёт в восемна́дцать часо́в?

18.00	News

2 Что идёт в два́дцать оди́н час?

3 Что идёт в девятна́дцать часо́в де́сять мину́т?

4 Что идёт в восемна́дцать часо́в два́дцать пять мину́т?

5 Что идёт в два́дцать два часа́ два́дцать мину́т?

6 Что идёт в два́дцать оди́н час три́дцать мину́т?

7 Что идёт в восемна́дцать пятна́дцать?

6 ⌦ Now listen to your recording again. A television announcer is giving the programmes for the evening. The announcement finishes with «передаём после́дние изве́стия» — 'here is the latest news'. Listen for the following information:

1	What is showing at 18.00?
2	When is the football match?
3	What is showing at 21.15?
4	What is showing at 21.45?

In Moscow the usual way of finding out about theatre and film programmes is from placards in the street (see illustration). There is also a weekly guide called Театра́льно-конце́ртная Москва́, which has more details, giving lists of the casts of the various productions, curtain times, etc. It is usual for theatres in Moscow to have a number of productions running at the same time, and, indeed, ten or so plays could be on the current programme. Nearly all evening performances of theatre, ballet and opera start at 7.00 p.m. This is often only indicated on the ticket by the word ве́чер (evening).

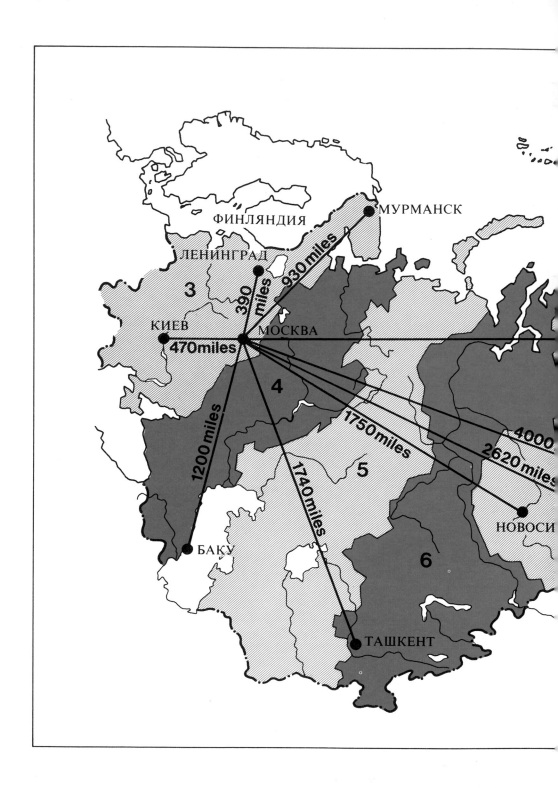

ФИНЛЯНДИЯ

МУРМАНСК

ЛЕНИНГРАД

3

КИЕВ

МОСКВА

470miles

390 miles

930 miles

4

1200 miles

1750miles

1740miles

5

4000

2620 miles

НОВОСИ

БАКУ

6

ТАШКЕНТ

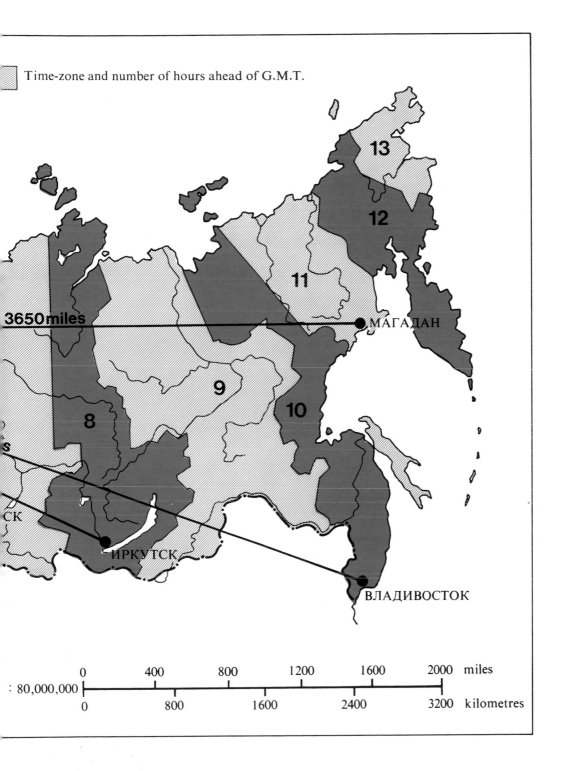

Time-zone and number of hours ahead of G.M.T.

13

12

11

3650 miles ● МАГАДАН

9

8 10

СК

ИРКУТСК

● ВЛАДИВОСТОК

: 80,000,000

| 0 | 400 | 800 | 1200 | 1600 | 2000 | miles |

| 0 | 800 | 1600 | 2400 | 3200 | kilometres |

7  Decipher the illustrated written forms, and print the words beneath the illustrations.

Summary

You should now be able to recognise verbs and to use some of them in the first person **Я** (*I*) and the second person **Вы/ты** (*you*). You have also met ways of saying you like things and have come across по in several of its many uses. You should also be able to recognise most times on the 24-hour clock.

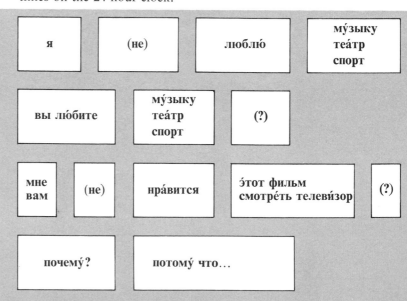

9

Eating and drinking

Going to a restaurant in the Soviet Union can be an interesting experience. Many of the best restaurants in Moscow have regional food, e.g. **Арáгви** *Georgian*, **Бакý** *Azerbaijani*, **Пекúн** *Chinese*, **Узбекистáн** *Central Asian*, **Минск** *White Russian*. Restaurants are often very busy, so it is as well to reserve a table. If you do this through Intourist, you will normally have to pay in foreign currency, often for a set menu (**дегустáция**). You could try going to the restaurant yourself.

If you manage to order a table in advance, you might save yourself the trouble of having to stand in a *queue* (**óчередь**). If you are in a restaurant or cafe and you want to know whether a place is free, simply ask the question **здесь свобóдно?** The answer might be

simply «**Да**» or «**свобóдно**» or «**садúтесь, пожáлуйста**» *please sit down*. Reasons why you might not be able to get into a restaurant may be as follows:

Ресторáн закры́т (на ремóнт)
                     (на учёт — *stocktaking*)
Здесь делегáция *or* у нас сегóдня делегáция
свáдьба *wedding*
Сегóдня приём *reception*
Ресторáн рабóтает тóлько с 4 до 10 часóв
Все местá зáняты *all the seats are taken* or simply
Мест нет!

When you have taken your seat in the restaurant, the waitress will ask you what you want. She might say **Слýшаю вас** *I'm at your service* and when she gives you food she might say **кýшайте на здорóвье!** (lit. *eat for the good of your health*).

Кýшать is a word often used by waitresses for *to eat*. It is never used in the first person 'I'. A more usual word for *to eat* is **есть**.

A way of saying *I am hungry* is **я хочý есть** (lit. *I want to eat*). **Я хочý пить** means *I want to drink*, i.e. *I'm thirsty*.* You know from unit 6 that the short way of asking for something is **у вас есть**… **борщ, бифштéкс, щи?** etc. Or you might say **дáйте, пожáлуйста**… or **мне, пожáлуйста,**… You also might want to know how much something (e.g. caviare) is, in which case you might ask **Скóлько стóит икрá?** **Дóрого** *expensive* might be your reply, especially if you're talking about black caviare. **Крáсная икрá не так дóрого стóит.**

* **я хочý** on its own means *I want*: **я хочý борщ, я не хочý кóфе**. You might use it to reply to the question: **Что вы хотúте?** *What do you want?*

68

1 ◾ Four people (**A**, **B**, **C**, **D**) are in a restaurant. They make their orders as listed below. You have to look at the menu, find the price for each item, write down the price in the space provided and then add them to get the total in each case. **Оди́н рубль = 100 копе́ек.**

	р	к			р	к
A Cocktail		_____	**B** Vodka		_____
Sardines		_____	Moscow salad		_____
Beetroot soup		_____	Cabbage soup		_____
Beefsteak		_____	Entrecote steak		_____
Stewed fruit		_____	Wine (red)		_____
Brandy		_____	Tea		_____
		======			======

	р	к			р	к
C Mineral water		_____	**D** Tomato juice		_____
Cabbage soup		_____	Crab salad		_____
Shashlyk		_____	Mushrooms in smetana		_____
Fruit		_____	Carp with mushrooms		_____
Coffee		_____	Mousse		_____
Lemonade		_____	Champagne		_____
		======	Tea with lemon		_____
					======

МЕНЮ́

Супы́, заку́ски		Вторы́е блю́да		Напи́тки	
щи	0.40 к.	карп жа́реный	1р.00 к.	во́дка	1р.45 к.
борщ	0.50 к.	карп с гриба́ми	1р.25 к.	конья́к	1р.45 к.
суп карто́фельный,	0.30 к.	антреко́т	1р.75 к.	шампа́нское	4р.00 к.
мясно́й	0.35 к.	филе́ «ко́смос»	1р.80 к.	вино́ (бе́лое)	3р.00 к.
суп с кукуру́зой	0.27 к.	шашлы́к	1р.85 к.	вино́ (кра́сное)	3р.50 к.
суп с гриба́ми	0.33 к.	котле́ты с гриба́ми	1р.50 к.	кокте́йль «конья́к»	2р.30 к.
огурцы́ со смета́ной	0.70 к.	котле́ты «министе́рство»	2р.00 к.	пунш	1р.80 к.
грибы́ в смета́не	1р.24 к.	бифште́кс натура́льный	2р.10 к.	лимона́д	0.21 к.
сарди́ны в ма́сле	0.80 к.	**Сла́дкие**		вода́ минера́льная	0.22 к.
сала́т моско́вский	0.75 к.	желе́ лимо́нное	0.20 к.	сок тома́тный	0.29 к.
сала́т мясно́й	0.70 к.	компо́т	0.25 к.	ко́фе	0.12 к.
сала́т «здоро́вье»	0.72 к.	фру́кты	0.30 к.	чай	0.08 к.
сала́т с кра́бами	0.78 к.	пу́динг	0.10 к.	чай (с лимо́ном)	0.14 к.
		мусс	0.12 к.		
		моро́женое	0.40 к.		

2  Listen to your recording. Four people decide to go to a restaurant. Although they have a little difficulty deciding what they want, since some dishes are 'off', eventually they finish up with the meals on page 69. You first hear them outside a restaurant in the centre of Moscow, discussing where to go and eat.

1	What is the name of the first restaurant they try?
2	Why can't they get in there?
3	Where do they decide to go?
4	How long do they have to stand in the queue?
5	Which of the dishes are off?

Black caviare **чёрная икра́** is the hard roe from the *sturgeon* **осётр** and is more prized than the cheaper **кра́сная икра́** which comes from Pacific salmon. Caviare can come from other fish, such as pike or zander, but these are not as popular as the usual varieties. *Fish* **ры́ба** plays a great part in the diet of the Russians and they tend to eat a much greater variety than we do, especially of freshwater fish. The common sea fish are found in coastal areas in the north, but not so frequently in Moscow. The ones you are likely to find in Moscow are **сельдь** *salted herring*, **шпро́ты** *sprats* and other preserved or tinned fish. Russians often eat freshwater fish which are sometimes sold live in the kolkhoz markets, and in special fish shops.

Here are some other dishes you might see on a menu.

Ку́рица (ку́ра)	*Chicken*
Инде́йка	*Turkey*
Ветчина́	*Ham*
Яйцо́	*Egg*
Яи́чница	*Egg dish* often fried with ham (usually available in a Буфе́т — good bet for breakfast).
Мя́со	*Meat*

Russians are very proud of their *ice-cream* **моро́женое**. It is sold all the year round on the streets.

3 📖 Look at the following picture. Put the numbers in the correct boxes.

чёрная икра́	☐	бе́лое вино́	☐	ку́рица	☐	фру́кты	☐	ры́ба ☐
вода́	☐	сала́т	☐	шашлы́к	☐	ко́фе	☐	моро́женое ☐

Whether in a restaurant or a Russian home, you will always find *bread* **хлеб** on the table. There is a wide variety of bread, but the ones which will appear as a matter of routine are **бе́лый хлеб** and **чёрный хлеб**. If you want to order *bread and butter*, ask for **хлеб с ма́слом**.

4 📼 Listen to your recording once more.

Our four friends are just finishing their meal. One of them calls the waitress; she asks them if they want anything else (**Что ещё?**) but all they want is *the bill* (**счёт**). Notice the use of the word **сейча́с** *right away*, immediately. This word means also 'I'll be with you in a moment' — but it frequently takes rather longer. Be patient! Russians tend to make an evening out of a meal, and there is usually dancing to a live orchestra.

The waitress asks them about the dishes. The shashlýk was *tasty* **вку́сный** but the carp was *not quite so nice* **не так вку́сный**.

The four friends pay separately and the waitress tots up their bills separately. She asks them what they had and writes down the sums on the bill. She then says **С вас**... and the amount and then moves to the next person who asks **Ско́лько с меня́?** *How much do you want from me?* The last one asks for *a packet of filter-tip cigarettes*

71

сигаре́ты с фи́льтром and *a box of matches* **спи́чки** and pays for them separately. Fill in the prices below:

		P.	Коп.
a	Ско́лько с меня́? С вас		
b	Ско́лько с меня́? С вас		
c	Ско́лько с меня́? С вас		
d	Ско́лько с меня́? С вас		
(Сигаре́ты с фи́льтром и спи́чки)			

The person in charge in a hotel or restaurant is usually referred to as **администра́тор** (male or female). This is the person to whom requests or complaints should be made. The *waitress* **официа́нтка** is there to serve you and if you complain she will usually refer you to the **администра́тор**. Tipping is officially frowned upon in the Soviet Union, but taxi drivers and waitresses will often gladly accept tips, and presents will be well received by persons responsible for making your stay in the USSR a comfortable one.

5 Decipher the illustrated written forms and print them in the boxes provided.

Summary

You should now know a few more ways of asking for things and a few more things you might want to ask for. One of the most useful expressions in this unit is **хочу́** *I want* — but don't forget to say **пожа́луйста**.

да́йте, мне,	пожа́луйста,	хлеб ко́фе моро́женое
что вы хоти́те? а вам что?	я хочу	хлеб ко́фе
ско́лько с меня́?	с вас 3р 50к	

10 Revision

This unit consists mainly of a series of exercises for revising the language you have learned so far. There is very little new vocabulary and only one new structure нýжно (necessary) as in Что вам нýжно? Мне нýжно купи́ть кóфе, i.e. I need... and это не то, что мне нýжно: that's not what I need. Here is a dialogue which takes place in a shop. The new words are translated in the margin.

ТУРИ́СТ — Здрáвствуйте.
ДЕ́ВУШКА — Здрáвствуйте

new brands Т — У вас есть **нóвые мáрки** фотоаппарáтов?

Д — Да, есть.

Т — Мóжно посмотрéть?

Д — Пожáлуйста. Вот хорóший совéтский аппарáт «Зени́т».

know...but Т — Я **зна́ю** о «Зени́те», **но** э́то не то, что мне ну́жно! Мо́жно посмотре́ть япо́нские ма́рки?

Д — Япо́нских аппара́тов у нас нет.

show Т — **Покажи́те**, пожа́луйста, вот э́тот.

German Д — (показывает) э́то но́вый **неме́цкий** аппара́т. О́чень хоро́ший.

Т — (смо́трит) Да. Ско́лько он сто́ит?

Д — 50 рубле́й.

will take...only come Т — Хм... Пожа́луй, **я его́ возьму́**... То́лько... Мо́жно **придти́**
to run...   watch за́втра? Сейча́с мне ну́жно **бежа́ть**... (смо́трит на **часы́**).

Д — Мо́жно.

Т — Спаси́бо! До свида́ния.

Д — Пожалуйста.

1 📖 👓 Answer these questions in English.

1	What does the man want?
2	What does the girl offer him?
3	What is his reply to this?
4	What does he finally decide on?
5	Why doesn't he take the camera straight away?

Now look at the following. It is a letter from a young visitor to Moscow to a girl who is in his class at school in Vladimir.*

Дорога́я О́ля!

hotel Вот я и в Москве́! У меня́ о́чень хоро́шая ко́мната в **гости́-
нице** «Росси́я» на Кра́сной пло́щади. У меня́ в ко́мнате есть
everything I need телеви́зор, ра́дио и телефо́н. **Всё, что ну́жно**. Сейча́с идёт амери-
main ка́нский фильм — о́чень хоро́ший фильм. **Гла́вную** роль игра́ет
о́чень краси́вая актри́са, англича́нка. Как дела́ у тебя́ до́ма? Как

* You will not be able to understand all the words, but you should be able to
extract the information necessary to answer the questions that follow.

папа и ма́ма? Моя́ ма́ма в Ленингра́де, а па́па рабо́тает в

writes Ирку́тске. Он о́чень лю́бит футбо́л и **пи́шет,** что игра́ет в те́ннис.

Пиши́! Мой а́дрес Москва́ К 9, гости́ница «Росси́я», ко́мната 524 Телефо́н — 298–65–24.

С приве́том,

Саша

2 📖 Answer the following questions. Put the appropriate letter in the box on the right.

1 **Где Са́ша?**

    А   В Кремле́

    Б   В гости́нице «Москва́»

    В   В гости́нице «Росси́я»

    Г   В теа́тре

2 **Где гости́ница?**

    А   В Ленингра́де

    Б   На у́лице Го́рького

    В   В Аме́рике

    Г   На Кра́сной пло́щади

3 **Что Са́ша сейча́с де́лает?**

    А   Гуля́ет по Москве́

    Б   Смо́трит фильм по телеви́зору

    В   Идёт в теа́тр

    Г   Идёт в хоро́ший рестора́н

4 **Что идёт по телеви́зору?**

    А   Америка́нский фильм

    Б   Фильм не о́чень интере́сный

    В   Игра́ет краси́вая англича́нка

    Г   Он не говори́т по-англи́йски

5 **Почему́ па́па в Ирку́тске?**

    А   Он смо́трит телеви́зор

    Б   Он там рабо́тает

    В   Он игра́ет в те́ннис

    Г   Он игра́ет в футбо́л.

3 Here is a matching exercise, using the time zone chart in Unit 8. This time the 24-hour clock is being used. For each item you are given the time in Moscow, and then asked what the time is in another town. The times you can choose from are on the clocks on the left. Place the number of the clock you choose in the appropriate box.

A Моско́вское вре́мя пятна́дцать часо́в. Кото́рый час в Ирку́тске?

B Моско́вское вре́мя двена́дцать часо́в. Кото́рый час во Владивосто́ке?

C Моско́вское вре́мя семна́дцать часо́в. Кото́рый час в Ташке́нте?

D Моско́вское вре́мя два́дцать часо́в. Кото́рый час в Ленингра́де?

E Моско́вское вре́мя шестна́дцать часо́в. Кото́рый час в Баку́?

F Моско́вское вре́мя шестна́дцать часо́в. Кото́рый час в Иркутске?

G Моско́вское вре́мя шестна́дцать часо́в. Кото́рый час в Магада́не?

4 Matching exercise. Turn to your recording. You will hear a number followed by a statement or question. Place the number you hear in the box next to the appropriate response below.

Два рубля́ 20 коп.

Хорошо́, а вы?

Нет, сейча́с закры́т.

Иди́те пря́мо, пото́м нале́во.

Нет, то́лько лимона́д.

Ничего́, а ты?

Здра́вствуйте, о́чень рад.

Нет, да́йте, пожа́луйста, ко́фе.

Нет, не хочу́. Я сего́дня за́нят.

Нет, не моя́.

Нет, да́йте пожа́луйста, чай.

Оля, приве́т! Как дела́?

5 📖 Look at the picture above and then answer the questions by supplying the missing word.

На _____ цветы́.

В ко́мнате _____ мужчи́ны и _____ .

Же́нщина говори́т _____ телефо́ну.

Оди́н мужчи́на _____ телеви́зор.

По телеви́зору _____ футбо́льный матч.

Many of the exercises, as you will have realised, are designed to help you get around Moscow on your own. Conducted tours will often include such places as the *Kremlin* (**Кремль**), **Мавзоле́й Ле́нина** (*Lenin Mausoleum*), **на Кра́сной пло́щади**, **Музе́й Ле́нина**, **ВДНХ**, **Центра́льный Музе́й Вооружённых Сил СССР** (*Military Museum*), etc. The centre of Moscow is full of museums. Most of the churches in the Kremlin have been turned into museums, and so has *St. Basil's Cathedral* **Храм Васи́лия Блаже́нного** sometimes called **Покро́вский собо́р**, on Red Square. Two of the most interesting museums are the **Оруже́йная пала́та** *Armoury*, which contains many precious objects from tsarist times, and the **Истори́ческий музе́й** *Historical Museum* on Red Square. There are also many beautiful churches and monasteries in the centre of Moscow. **Новоде́вичий монасты́рь**, where the church is still 'working', is one of the most beautiful. It has next to it a cemetery, where many famous Russians are buried, including **Го́голь**, **Че́хов**, **Алексе́й Толсто́й**, **Станисла́вский** and **Хрущёв**. *Art galleries* are also referred to as **Музе́й**.

The Pushkin Museum and the Tret'yakov Gallery are the two largest galleries in Moscow. The former has a large collection of western paintings, including Picasso and Matisse, and the Tret'yakov contains native Russian works, including a large number of ikons.

КРОССВО́РД

NOTE: This crossword consists mainly of words you already know or can easily guess. New or difficult words are marked with an asterisk in the clues, which are perhaps best attempted when other clues have been solved.

Clues Across

1. *Excuse me* = **извини́те** or _____
7. And
10. _____ о́чень нра́вится танцева́ть
12. 'Aha! Russian style
14. Ско́лько _____ э́та ша́пка?
16. Not the boxing kind of blow. More like a stunning drink.
17. Вам нра́вится _____ фильм?
19. But
20. This is what happens before you get thrown into gaol*
22. Same as 19
23. Акаде́мия Нау́к (*Academy of Sciences*)
24. In the Latvian capital = В _____
25. From*
27. — Как вы пожива́ете?
    — Спаси́бо _____ ок
29. So
33. Ива́н гуля́ет _____ Москве́
35. Как вам _____ Москва́?
36. Famous river in Росто́в with Cossack connections
37. Not
38. Short for О́льга
40. State Universal Store
41. Well, . . .
42. To go walking
44. Они́ *love* грибы́
50. You can drink пи́во here*
51. Russian choir (starts with X)
52. I'm for it = Я _____ (do this after 42 and 43 down)*
53. Volume or tome*
54. Моско́вское вре́мя двена́дцать

Clues Down

1. Slang for a priest but not for a Pope!*
2. В _____ о́чень хоро́шее меню́
3. East as in German*
4. Я _____ телеви́зор
5. Comrade
6. Moscow University
7. And
8. Not
9. Ten
11. Russian girl (from Argentina?)
13. Same as 23 across
15. Metric tonne (fem.)*
16. Prefix
18. _____ говоря́т о футбо́ле
21. _____ буфе́т откры́т в три часа́. (Not ВЧЕРА́ or ЗА́ВТРА)
22. Musical note (fem.)*
26. 9
28. Кото́рый _____? Четы́ре
30. Not breast-stroke (ends with a soft sign)
31. Э́то вход. — Мо́жно войти́?
32. Institute of Language (ЯЗЫ́К) and Literature (Initials)
33. Ива́н говори́т _____ -ру́сски
34. Ири́на студе́нтка. _____ рабо́тает в университе́те
39. Musical note 'A'. (Do 38 and 42 across first)
42. We get this from the North Sea
43. Russian hooray [GUESS!]
45. Short for Ю́рий
46. What the Russians (and the French) shout for ENCORE*
47. Short for 5 down
48. Short for Ири́на
49. Сего́дня _____ телеви́зору о́чень интере́сная програ́мма
50. Я хоте́л _____ a word you'll meet later (*see page 107*)

79

6  Here is a plan of the Moscow underground. How many changes do you need to make to complete a journey to each of the stations indicated in the list below? The starting point each time is the same, **Пло́щадь Револю́ции**, one of the nearest stations to Red Square. Make the least number of changes. To make the task easier we have divided the **СХЕ́МА** *Plan* into four parts: А, Б, В, Г and indicated which part the destination is in.

Starting point

Пло́щадь Револю́ции

Destination

ВДНХ (Б) ☐
Соко́льники (Б) ☐
Изма́йловский Парк (Б) ☐
Тага́нская (Г) ☐
Но́вые Черёмушки (В) ☐
Университе́т (В) ☐
Фили́ (В) ☐
Пу́шкинская (А) ☐
Дина́мо (А) ☐
Ле́нинские Го́ры (В) ☐

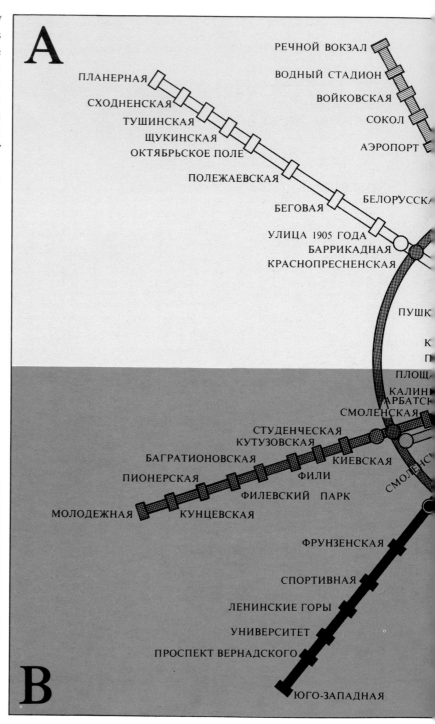

КИРОВСКО-ФРУНЗЕНСКАЯ ЛИНИЯ

АРБАТСКО-ПОКРОВСКАЯ ЛИНИЯ

ГОРЬКОВСКО-ЗАМОСКВОРЕЦКАЯ ЛИНИЯ

КОЛЬЦЕВАЯ ЛИНИЯ

КАЛУЖСКО-РИЖСКАЯ ЛИНИЯ

ФИЛЕВСКАЯ ЛИНИЯ

ЖДАНОВСКО-КРАСНОПРЕСНЕНСКАЯ ЛИНИЯ

СТАНЦИИ ПЕРЕСАДОК

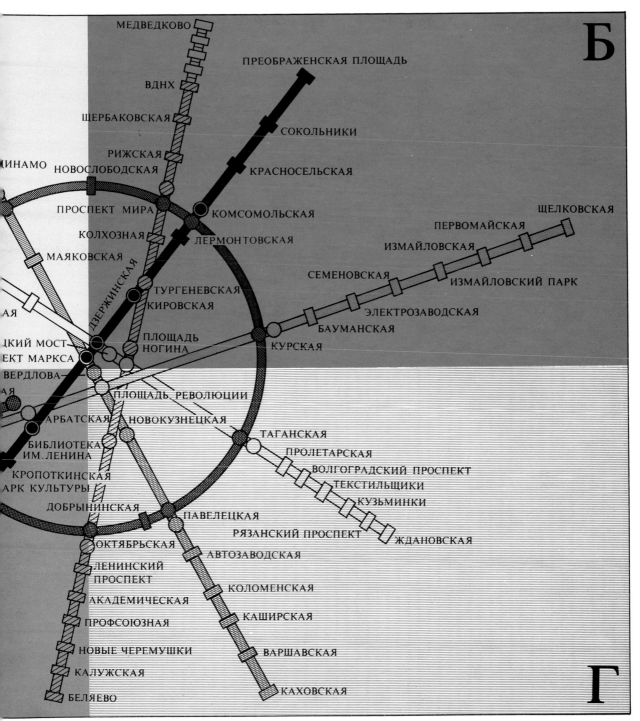

МЕДВЕДКОВО

ВДНХ

ЩЕРБАКОВСКАЯ

РИЖСКАЯ

ИНАМО НОВОСЛОБОДСКАЯ

ПРОСПЕКТ МИРА

КОЛХОЗНАЯ

МАЯКОВСКАЯ

КИЙ МОСТ
ЕКТ МАРКСА

ВЕРДЛОВА
АЯ

АРБАТСКАЯ

БИБЛИОТЕКА
ИМ. ЛЕНИНА

КРОПОТКИНСКАЯ
АРК КУЛЬТУРЫ

ДОБРЫНИНСКАЯ

ОКТЯБРЬСКАЯ

ЛЕНИНСКИЙ
ПРОСПЕКТ

АКАДЕМИЧЕСКАЯ

ПРОФСОЮЗНАЯ

НОВЫЕ ЧЕРЕМУШКИ

КАЛУЖСКАЯ

БЕЛЯЕВО

ПРЕОБРАЖЕНСКАЯ ПЛОЩАДЬ

СОКОЛЬНИКИ

КРАСНОСЕЛЬСКАЯ

КОМСОМОЛЬСКАЯ

ЛЕРМОНТОВСКАЯ

ТУРГЕНЕВСКАЯ

КИРОВСКАЯ

ПЛОЩАДЬ
НОГИНА

КУРСКАЯ

ПЛОЩАДЬ РЕВОЛЮЦИИ

НОВОКУЗНЕЦКАЯ

ТАГАНСКАЯ

ПРОЛЕТАРСКАЯ

ВОЛГОГРАДСКИЙ ПРОСПЕКТ

ТЕКСТИЛЬЩИКИ

КУЗЬМИНКИ

ПАВЕЛЕЦКАЯ

РЯЗАНСКИЙ ПРОСПЕКТ

ЖДАНОВСКАЯ

АВТОЗАВОДСКАЯ

КОЛОМЕНСКАЯ

КАШИРСКАЯ

ВАРШАВСКАЯ

КАХОВСКАЯ

ЩЕЛКОВСКАЯ

ПЕРВОМАЙСКАЯ

ИЗМАЙЛОВСКАЯ

СЕМЕНОВСКАЯ

ИЗМАЙЛОВСКИЙ ПАРК

ЭЛЕКТРОЗАВОДСКАЯ

БАУМАНСКАЯ

ДЗЕРЖИНСКАЯ

Б

Г

81

11

Time: days, dates and the future

1979
МАЙ

ПН.		7	14	21	28
ВТ.	1	8	15	22	29
СР.	2	9	16	23	30
ЧТ.	3	10	17	24	31
ПТ.	4	11	18	25	
СБ.	5	12	19	26	
ВС.	6	13	20	27	

See Grammar notes
page 155

The days of the week (дни недéли) are as follows, starting with Monday, as is usual in Russian calendars:

понедéльник
втóрник
средá
четвéрг
пя́тница
суббóта
воскресéнье

Какóй сегóдня день? (What day is it today?)	Сегóдня	средá суббóта пя́тница воскресéнье

You may recognise the beginnings of some of them — **втóр/ник** (**втор/óй** *second*), **чет/вéрг** (**четвёртый** *fourth*), **пя́т/ница** (**пя́тый** *fifth*). **Суббóта** is similar to the Jewish *Sabbath* and **воскресéнье** is derived from the Russian word for *Resurrection*, **воскресéние**, which is also the title of a novel by Lev Tolstoy. The prefix **вос-** (or **вс-** or **вз-**) usually means movement in an upwards direction, e.g. **вставáть** — (**встаю́, встаёшь, встаёт**, etc. *to get up*, **восстáние** *uprising*, **взлёт** *take-off, etc.*).

Months look very much like English ones, since both have a common (Latin) origin. You should be able to work out what they are.

янвáрь феврáль	зимá *winter*	ию́нь ию́ль áвгуст	лéто *summer*
март апрéль май	веснá *spring*	сентя́брь октя́брь ноя́брь	óсень *autumn*
		декáбрь —	зимá

Notice that days, months and seasons all start with a small letter.

If you want to say 'on Monday', 'on Tuesday' etc., simply put в in front of the word or во in the case of вто́рник (Tuesday). The -a endings change to -y.

Examples:

в понеде́льник
в воскресе́нье
во вто́рник
в пя́тницу
в суббо́ту

With months, the endings change to -e:

в	январе́	*in January*
в	ма́рте	*in March*
в	ию́ле	*in July*
в	декабре́	*in December*

83

Notice that the stress is on the end in the last example. This happens in all the autumn and winter months ending in -ь but not in the spring and summer months (**в апре́ле** but **в январе́**).

Seasons don't need a separate word to indicate 'in'. They simply change the endings:

зимо́й — *in winter*

весно́й — *in spring*

ле́том — *in summer*

о́сенью — *in autumn*

A similar thing occurs with times of the day:

у́тро	*morning*	у́тром	*in the morning*
день	*day*	днём	*during the day*
ве́чер	*evening*	ве́чером	*in the evening*
ночь	*night*	но́чью	*at night*

See Grammar notes (Instrumental) page 155

Како́е сего́дня число́? Сего́дня пя́тое января́
What date is it today? Сего́дня пе́рвое ма́рта

Notice that the ending on the month changes to **-я** or **-a**. Here are some headings from **Театра́льно-конце́ртная Москва́**, the weekly

84

guide. The first two are for the **Кремлёвский Дворец Съездов**, *the Kremlin Palace of Congresses*, the largest auditorium in Moscow.

Пятница 17 февраля	Понедельник 20 февраля	Четверг 16 февраля
ЧИО-ЧИО-САН	**КОППЕЛИЯ**	**ПИКОВАЯ ДАМА**
Опера в 3 действиях Музыка **Д. Пуччини** Либретто **Л. Иллика** и **Д. Джакоза**	Балет в 3 действиях Музыка **Л. Делиба** Либретто **Ш. Ньютерра, А. Сен-Леона** Новая редакция **А. Кузнецова** и **А. Радунского**	Опера в 3 действиях Музыка **П. И. Чайковского** Либретто **М. И. Чайковского** по повести **А. С. Пушкина**

1 ◣ Look at the dates below. Put in the number of the month after the day. The first one is done for you.

	Day FRI	*Date* 16	*Month* 6
пя́тница, шестна́дцатое ию́ня	FRI	16	6
вто́рник, деся́тое ноября́			
понеде́льник, два́дцать пя́тое апре́ля			
суббо́та, пе́рвое ию́ля			
среда́, тридца́тое декабря́			

If you want to say the time when something will take place, an easy way of doing it is by simply using the word бу́дет. Here are some examples.

Матч бу́дет в пя́тницу — *The match will be (take place) on Friday.*
Фильм бу́дет за́втра в 8 часо́в — *The film will be on tomorrow at 8 o'clock.*
Бале́т бу́дет за́втра ве́чером в 7 часо́в — *The ballet will be tomorrow night, at 7 o'clock.*

Я бу́ду *I shall be*, **мы бу́дем** *we shall be* may also be used in this way — **я бу́ду в рестора́не в шесть часо́в**, etc. Бу́ду, бу́дет, etc. can also be used in conjunction with a verb to indicate the future, e.g.

я	бу́ду рабо́тать	*I shall be working*
он	бу́дет чита́ть	*He will be reading*
вы	бу́дете гуля́ть	*You will be going for a walk*
мы	бу́дем обе́дать в час	*We shall be having lunch at one*

85

Обéд means lunch or dinner, and takes place any time between mid-day and about 5 o'clock. In Soviet households it is normally the main meal of the day. Meals taken before mid-day are usually referred to as **зáвтрак** *breakfast*. Children in schools often have **вторóй зáвтрак** lit. *second breakfast* at around 11 a.m. **Ýжин** *supper* is often a late evening meal. **До обéда** is *before lunch*; *after lunch* **пóсле обéда**. You will also hear **обéдать** *to have lunch*, **зáвтракать** *to have breakfast* and **ýжинать** *to have supper*.

2 ▱ Listen to your recording. A guide is describing to a group of tourists their itinerary for a stay in Moscow. They ask him questions about various events that are going to take place. You have the time-table in front of you, but, as you will see, there are gaps. Fill in the gaps using the information on the recording.

суббóта 8ᵒᵉ июля	08.00–09.10	зáвтрак
	_____	экскýрсия по Москвé
	13.00	обéд
	14.30	_____
	_____	Большóй Теáтр
	_____	ýжин
воскресéнье _____	08.00–09.00	зáвтрак
	10.00	экскýрсия по Кремлю́
	13.00	_____
	14.00	Истори́ческий Музéй и Мавзолéй Лéнина
	_____	ВДНХ
	22.00	ýжин
понедéльник 10ᵒᵉ июля	_____	зáвтрак
departure	08.00	**отъéзд** в Ленингрáд

86

Opening and closing times of Russian shops are much more flexible than in the West.

Many Russians are shift workers and some food shops have extended opening hours in the evening. Lunch hours tend to vary from shop to shop and if you decide to return to a shop in a few days' time to make a purchase, it might save irritation if you make a note of the **обéденный перерыв** *lunch hour* and the **выходнóй день** *closing* *See below* *day*. The times are nearly always posted in the window of the shop. There is always a chance that when you return the shop will be closed **на ремóнт** or **на учёт** or that there will be a **санитáрный день** *cleaning day* but you'll have to take a chance on that!

3 ◗ This is the sort of notice you might see in a shop. Read through it and then answer the questions in English.

Магазúн рабóтает

Пн	с	8.00 часóв до	19.00ч.
Вт		10.00	21.00
Ср		9.00	20.00
Чт		9.00	20.00
Пт		9.00	20.00
Сб		9.00	12.00
Вс		выходнóй	

обéденный перерыв 13.00–14.00ч.

1	Which day does the shop open late?
2	Which is the closing day?
3	What time does the shop open on Wednesdays?
4	When is the lunch break?
5	Which day does the shop close early?

Writing Russian (i)

Some Russian letters are written exactly as you would expect, but if you wish to learn to write, beware of using English variations, as many of these would not be understood by a Russian. In the examples below, you will be given the letters which are difficult or new. You should assume that the other letters are as you would expect them to be. *Check your answers in the margin below.* Capital letters are given in brackets.

T is written *m̄* (*Ⲧ*) or *т* and И is written *и* (*Ⲩ*)

        write такси _____

П is written *п* (*Ⲡ*) write парк _____

Н is written *н* (*Ⲏ*) write пианист _____

В is written *в* (*Ⲃ*) write а́виа _____

Summary

You should now be able to recognise all the days of the week, months of the year, seasons and times of the day. You should also be able to recognise and use the future tense of 'to be' буду, etc. and the future of verbs with буду + infinitive.

какой сегодня день?		

сегодня	среда́ суббо́та пя́тница	

какое сегодня число?		

сегодня	пя́тое января́ пе́рвое ма́рта	

я бу́ду	гуля́ть рабо́тать	?
вы бу́дете		

такси

парк

пианист

88 *авиа*

12

What was and what will be

So far in the course we have been using the present tense (**рабо́таю** *I am working, I work*; **чита́ю** *I am reading, I read*) and the future **я бу́ду** (**рабо́тать**) — *I shall* (*work*), *shall be* (*working*), *etc.*; **я бу́ду** (**чита́ть**) — *I shall* (*read*), *shall be* (*reading*), *etc.* In this unit we are going to look at the past, to compare the past with the future. Look at the following examples.

See Grammar notes (Verbs) page 160

Вы за́втра бу́дете в Ки́еве? *Will you be in Kiev tomorrow?*
Нет, я был там вчера́. *No, I was there yesterday.*

Она́ за́втра бу́дет в Ленингра́де?
Нет, она́ была́ там вчера́.

Они́ за́втра бу́дут в Москве́?
Нет, они́ бы́ли там вчера́.

You will deduce that the verb ending for the past is in '-л' for 'он' nouns, '-ла' for 'она' nouns (for 'оно' nouns it would be '-ло') and '-ли' for plurals, i.e. you take чита́ть, говори́ть, быть, etc., take off -ть and add the endings as follows:

See Grammar notes (Infinitives) page 160

Ви́ктор чита́л кни́гу
Студе́нтка рабо́тала
Кафе́ бы́ло закры́то
Ви́тя и О́ля говори́ли о спо́рте   etc.

Look at the following passage and note the **past tenses**.

В про́шлом году́ *last year* я **был** в Москве́. Пого́да *weather* там **была́** о́чень хоро́шая. Мы **жи́ли** в гости́нице «Росси́я» в це́нтре Москвы́. Я ча́сто **ходи́л** по го́роду. Не́сколько раз *several times* я **смотре́л** футбо́льный матч. Одна́жды **игра́ли** «Дина́мо» Москва́ и «Дина́мо» Ки́ев. По́сле э́того ма́тча мы **поу́жинали** в гости́нице, а пото́м **потанцева́ли**. Мне ну́жно **бы́ло** рабо́тать ка́ждый день. Я **рабо́тал** в **библиоте́ке**, где **чита́л** интере́сные кни́ги.

library

You will notice that some of the past forms above have по- on the beginning. This usually indicates that the action is complete. Other prefixes also occur, but по- is the most common.

See Grammar notes (Aspects) page 161

89

1 📖 Look at the diary below. It is written by a girl student, О́льга, at Moscow University (студе́нтка в Моско́вском Университе́те). Notice the endings of the verbs.

14ᵒᵉ мая

Сего́дня я вста́ла в 7 часо́в. Поза́втракала в буфе́те. На за́втрак бы́ли ко́фе и яи́чница. По́сле обе́да была́ в библиоте́ке, чита́ла газе́ты. Ве́чером смотре́ла фильм «Чёрная берёза». Фильм мне о́чень понра́вился.

15ᵒᵉ мая

У́тром сиде́ла в ко́мнате и чита́ла кни́гу по фи́зике. Пото́м написа́ла письмо́ па́пе. Пообе́дала в столо́вой, ела́ шашлы́к. По́сле обе́да купи́ла грибы́ на колхо́зном ры́нке. За́втра бу́дет экза́мен по фи́зике. Ну́жно рабо́тать!

16ᵒᵉ мая

Сдала экза́мен, получи́ла 4. Брат (Ви́тя) пи́шет, что бу́дет рабо́тать в колхо́зе. А я ду́мала, что он бу́дет учи́ться здесь, в Москве́.

Answer the questions in English

1	What did Ol′ga have for breakfast on 14th May?
2	What did she do in the evening?
3	What subject is she studying?
4	What did she buy at the колхоз market?
5	Where is her brother going to work?

Колхо́з is an abbreviation of **коллекти́вное хозя́йство** — *collective farm*. Land was nationalised in the Soviet Union after the Revolution and belongs to the State. It is let in perpetuity to the collective farms, which pay taxes in kind to the State. Collective farmers normally have their own smallholdings on which they grow their own produce. What they do not consume themselves they sell at the **колхо́зный ры́нок** *kolkhoz market*. **Совхо́з** (сове́тское

хозяйство) is also *a farm*, usually much larger than a **колхо́з**, and is owned by the State. These are on the increase.

Russians are very conscious of their historical identity and everywhere you go in the Soviet Union you will find monuments, plaques, and historical museums. Moscow is particularly rich in these. Besides the **Истори́ческий Музе́й** *Historical Museum* in Red Square and the Lenin Museum, there is a *Museum of the Revolution* **Музе́й Револю́ции**. Many museums are devoted to famous historical and literary personalities. Here are some of them.

Музе́й А. М. Го́рького, ул. Воро́вского д. 25
Музе́й Ф. М. Достое́вского, ул. Достое́вского д. 2
Музе́й А. С. Пу́шкина, Кропо́ткинская ул. д. 12
Музе́й Л. Н. Толсто́го, Кропо́ткинская ул. д. 11

Many of these museums are housed in places where the people concerned lived and worked, and, if you are interested in literature, you will find them well worth a visit. The above list is by no means complete. Another interesting museum is devoted to **Маяко́вский** Mayakovsky, a famous post-revolutionary poet whose statue stands on one of the main squares off Gorky Street. In fact, Moscow has an abundance of statues to literary and historical figures — Pushkin, Gógol', Marx, Engels and others too numerous to mention. Perhaps one of the most interesting is the monument to **Ю́рий Долгору́кий** *Yury 'Long-hand'*, the founder of Moscow, also off Gorky Street.

Another thing that the visitor will notice is the presence on the sides of buildings of plaques telling of some historical event that took place at that spot. This is the sort of thing you might see;

An unusual plaque in Leningrad is:–

(*This side of the street is more dangerous during artillery bombardment.*)

This dates back to the siege of Leningrad during World War II.   93

The most important historical event for Russians is, of course, the October Revolution and many Russians often compare things *before the Revolution* до Револю́ции with things *after the Revolution* по́сле Револю́ции.

2 ■ Here is a list of some of the main dates in Russian history. The questions at the end are designed to help you understand the text. Use them to work out the vocabulary.

Гла́вные да́ты ру́сской исто́рии

860–1240	Ки́евская Русь
1113–1125	Влади́мир Монома́х, Князь (Ки́ев)
1147	Основа́ние Москвы́
1223	Чинги́з-хан и монго́льская а́рмия разби́ли слав-я́нскую а́рмию
1227	Смерть Чинги́з-ха́на.
1240–1480	Тата́рское и́го
1326	Москва́ ста́ла полити́ческим це́нтром Руси́
1533–1584	Ива́н IV (Ива́н Гро́зный) стал царём в 1547 году́
1598–1605	Бори́с Годуно́в, царь
1682–1725	Пётр I (Пётр Вели́кий) царь
1697–1698	Пётр на За́паде, в Голла́ндии и в А́нглии
1703	Основа́ние Санкт-Петербу́рга
1762–1796	Екатери́на II
1812–1814	Оте́чественная война́ с Наполео́ном
1861	Крестья́нская рефо́рма (освобожде́ние крестья́н)
1905	Револю́ция 1905 го́да
1914	Начала́сь Пе́рвая мирова́я война́
1917	Февра́льская Револю́ция
	Октя́брьская Револю́ция
1918–1922	Гражда́нская война́
1924	Смерть Ле́нина
1953	Смерть Ста́лина
1941–1945	Вели́кая Оте́чественная война́

1 When was Vladimir Monomakh prince of Kiev?

2 When was the founding of Moscow?

3 When did Ghengiz Khan defeat the Slav army?

4 When did he die?

94

5	What were the years of the Tartar yoke?	
6	When did Moscow become the political centre of Rus'?	
7	Against whom was the 'War of the Fatherland' in 1812?	
8	When was the peasant reform?	
9	When did the First World War start?	
10	When did the October Revolution take place?	
11	When did Lenin die?	
12	When did Stalin die?	

Photographs of old Moscow

КРОССВО́РД

Now here is a crossword. Many of the answers are historical. Some of these occur in the list above. Some words are new. Many of these you will be able to guess, especially if you solve the associated clues first. *Answers on p. 173.*

Across

1   Not
3   Moscow State University
5   Tolstoy's first name (ends in Й)
8   Leningrad Committee (abbrev.)
9   Great Russian Tsar
11 Jelly (*see menu page 69*)
12 Мы жи́ли там не́сколько _____
    _____. (*Genitive plural of* ЛЕ́ТО)
14 This is on an airmail letter
17 Japanese camera and Russian Patriarch before Peter the Great
18 Great English playwright
20 Алма́-_____. Го́род в СССР
21 Pushkin wrote a story called 'The Arab of Peter the Great'. Its Russian title is _____ Петра́ Вели́кого.
23 Khrushchev's first name
26 Polish landowner or 'sir'.
28 Short comrade
30 What 5 down was called — до револю́ции
32 Chinese leader
33 It sounds like support for ladies in Russia, but it isn't! It's a wall lamp
35 And
36 Чинги́з-_____. The leader of the Golden Horde
37 To go on foot
38 Initially Брита́нский Конгре́сс Тредюнио́нов

Down

2   Her
3   Ministry of Trade (Министе́р-ство Торго́вли)
4   Already
5   City built by Peter for Lenin?
6   Century
7   Reorganised by Peter the Great. Fleet but not of foot.
8   Russian river and girl's name. Lenin took his name from this area
9   Ballet step as in French
10 Great Russian lover? They say poison couldn't kill him
13 Town to the south of Moscow, near Tolstoy's estate
15 Girl's name
16 Executive (Исполни́тельный) Committee
18 What Russians wear on their heads in winter
19 Го́род в Ита́лии, где живёт Па́па
22 Russian cream (e.g. for shaving)
24 Дина́мо, Торпе́до, for instance.
25 What the ancient inhabitants of 19 down wore
27 The river in 5 down
29 There you are!
30 Russian fluff — 'y' is the middle letter
31 Peter the Great used to sail an англи́йский _____ .
34 Republican Library (abbrev.)

Writing Russian (ii)

You must be careful of the height of the letters. There are fewer letters which go above and below the line in Russian. This gives printed and written Russian a different profile from English, and it takes a while to adjust to this.

Д   is written *g* or *д* (*Д*)   write во́дка _____

З   is written *з* (*З*)   write зоопа́рк _____

                                        write Пра́вда _____

                                        write университе́т _____

Х   is written *х* (*Х*)   write хокке́й _____

Г   is written *г* (*Г*)   write го́род _____

Summary

You should now know something about the Russian past, in historical and linguistic terms. Much of the historical vocabulary is very similar to English, so it will be easy for you to remember.

быть	:	я был она́ была́ они́ бы́ли	там вчера́
быть	:	я бу́ду она бу́дет они бу́дут	там за́втра

во́дка
зоопа́рк
Пра́вда
университет
хокке́й
го́род

13

Getting around: transport

You have already met one word for going on foot идти — идёт, пойдём, etc. Russians make a distinction between going on foot (идти) and going by vehicle (éхать). You will come across these words in many forms. Here are some of them:

Идите — *Walk* (Signal at a pedestrian crossing)
Как проéхать в/до...? *How do I travel to...?*
Я хочý поéхать в... *I want to get* (travel) *to...*

See Grammar notes page 160

Public road transport in Moscow and other cities is often very crowded and passengers cooperate with one another by passing their money down the bus for the person nearest to the **автомáт** *ticket machine* to put in the money and tear off tickets. If you find yourself not having access to the machine, the phrase you will need is **передáйте, пожáлуйста** *please pass it on*. People who have books of tickets will punch them, using a machine on the wall. They might well ask you to punch their ticket for them. People wanting to get past you will ask you if you are going to get off at the next stop '**Вы сейчáс выхóдите?**' or '**Вы выхóдите на слéдующей?**'. They might also say '**Пропустите, пожáлуйста**' '*Let me through, please*'. The driver will usually tell you what the next stop is '**Слéдующая останóвка...**'. You will need to listen carefully for this.

On the underground the announcement to listen for is '**Осто-рóжно, двéри закрывáются. Слéдующая останóвка**…'. '*Careful, the doors are closing. The next stop is…*'.

1  Listen to the recording, and answer the questions which follow.

The first part of the dialogue takes place on a bus, the second part on the Metro. Use the plan of the Metro on *page 80* to help you. Answer the following questions in English.

1	Which is the next bus stop?
2	Where does the lady want to get off?
3	Which stop does the man get off?
4	Where does he get off in the Metro?
5	Using the Metro scheme, find out where he boarded.

2 ▄Sometimes, of course, you have to change from one form of transport to another, or change trains on the Metro. This is called a **пересáдка** and you can either travel **с пересáдкой** *with a change* or **без пересáдки** *without a change, straight through.* Here are some possible routes. You have to decide, using the **схéма** on *pages 80–81,* whether the journey is with or without a change, and add the appropriate ending to the word **пересáдка**. If there is a change (**с пересáдкой**) write down the name of the station where the change takes place. If not, (**без пересáдки**), write down the number of stops to the destination. The first two are done for you.

	от (стáнции)	до (стáнции)		
1	Динáмо	→ Кúевская	~~без~~/с* пересáдкой	**Белорýсская**
2	Кропóткинская	→ Университéт	без/~~с~~* пересáдки	**пять**
3	Университéт	→ Библиотéка им. Лéнина	без/с* пересáдк...	_____
4	Профсоюзная	→ Тагáнская	без/с* пересáдк...	_____
5	Автозавóдская	→ Сокóльники	без/с* пересáдк...	_____
6	Кýрская	→ Краснопрéсненская	без/с* пересáдк...	_____
7	Нóвые Черёмушки	→ Парк Культýры	без/с* пересáдк...	_____
8	Комсомóльская	→ ВДНХ	без/с* пересáдк...	_____
9	Арбáтская	→ Первомáйская	без/с* пересáдк...	_____
10	Плóщадь Револю́ции	→ Смолéнская	без/с* пересáдк...	_____
11	Филú	→ Октя́брьская	без/с* пересáдк...	_____
12	Югозáпадная	→ Кúровская	без/с* пересáдк...	_____

* delete as appropriate

A form of transport rare in this country but common in the Soviet Union is the *fixed route taxi* — **маршрýтное таксú** '*minibuses*' which hold about a dozen people. They cost **дéсять копéек** *ten kopeks* any distance but will only stop at points along their fixed routes.

Distances in the Soviet Union are very great. Many train journeys are made overnight, and if you want to go to the Far East — **Владивосто́к**, for example — the journey can take up to a week. Sleeping cars are standard, with four or six to a compartment in the **жёсткий** *hard* **ваго́н**, and two or four to a compartment in the **мя́гкий** *soft* **ваго́н**. Each carriage is looked after by a **проводни́к** *attendant* or **проводни́ца** if it's a woman, who usually has a water heater going in case you want a glass of tea. You will be charged a few kopeks, or its equivalent in hard currency (if you are on a Russian train outside the USSR) for each glass you have. The **проводни́к** or **проводни́ца** will supply you with bedding. Usually Russians provide themselves with food for the journey, as eating in the restaurant cars can be expensive. Travelling is often treated as a social occasion — Russians like to get to know their travelling companions and frequently ask questions which may seem to the Westerner to be very direct, e.g. **Ско́лько вы получа́ете?** *What is your salary?* N.B. They usually mean *per month* (**в ме́сяц**). Far from being offended, feel free to ask similar questions yourself!

Trains are numbered in the Soviet Union, so on the railway **расписа́ние** *timetable* you will see the number of the train (№ по́езда), the **вре́мя отправле́ния** *time of departure* and the **прибы́тие** *time of arrival*.

Here is a situation in a main-line *railway station* **На вокза́ле.**

Спра́вочное бюро́

Тури́ст:	Скажи́те, пожа́луйста, где здесь ка́сса?
Де́вушка:	**Куда́** вы е́дете?
Тури́ст:	В Ленингра́д.
Де́вушка:	А когда́?
Тури́ст:	Сего́дня.
Де́вушка:	Ва́ша ка́сса бу́дет в большо́м за́ле, нале́во…
Тури́ст:	Спаси́бо.

Where to...

У биле́тной ка́ссы

Тури́ст:	Пожа́луйста, оди́н биле́т в Ленингра́д на сего́дня.
Де́вушка:	На како́й по́езд?
Тури́ст:	А каки́е есть поезда́?
Де́вушка:	Есть по́езд No. 12 в 6.30 ве́чера. Есть ещё оди́н, No. 3, в 23 часа́ 55 мин. Экспре́сс «Кра́сная Стрела́».
Тури́ст:	Так… (*ду́мает*) Мне ну́жно быть в Ленингра́де у́тром… Я пое́ду на 23.55… Когда́ я бу́ду в Ленингра́де?
Де́вушка:	В 8 утра́. Оди́н биле́т?
Тури́ст:	Да, пожа́луйста. Оди́н биле́т.
Де́вушка:	С вас 14 рубле́й 20 копе́ек. (*Тури́ст пла́тит.*)
Тури́ст:	Скажи́те, с како́й платфо́рмы бу́дет по́езд?
Де́вушка:	С пе́рвой.
Тури́ст:	Спаси́бо.

3 📖 📺 Fill in the gaps in the following sentences.

1   Мужчи́на хо́чет пое́хать в _____.

2   Поезда́ в _____ и в _____.

3   По́езд бу́дет в Ленингра́де _____.

4   Биле́т в Ленингра́д сто́ит _____.

5   По́езд отхо́дит с платфо́рмы но́мер _____.

Opposite is part of a timetable giving tariffs and travelling times (**тари́фы и вре́мя**) from Moscow, by plane (**самолётом***), and by train (**по́ездом**).

* You can also say автóбусом *by bus*, троллéйбусом *by trolleybus* or трамвáем *by tram. See Grammar notes (Instrumental case) page 155*

102

Пункт назначения (от Москвы)	Цена билета (руб. коп.)		Время в пути (час. мин.)	
	самолётом	в мягком вагоне поезда	самолётом	поездом
АЛМА-АТА	62	44.60	4.10	67.35
АРХАНГЕЛЬСК	24	20.20	1.45	18.37
АШХАБАД	54	42.60	3.40	69.35
БАКУ	40	32.20	2.40	42.09
БАЛХАШ	56	39.30	6.03	78.37
БАРНАУЛ	60	39.30	3.55	61.27
БАТУМИ	36	30.10	3.05	42.10
БЛАГОВЕЩЕНСК	116	81.10	11.25	143.10
БУГУЛЬМА	24	19.00	2.10	27.16
ВИЛЬНЮС	20	18.00	1.30	13.18
ВЛАДИВОСТОК	134	93.70	9.55	170.00
ВОЛГОГРАД	22	19.90	1.35	18.15
ВОЛОГДА	15	12.10	1.15	7.32
ВОРКУТА	42	29.60	2.55	38.57
ВОРОНЕЖ	15	12.90	1.10	10.20
ГОМЕЛЬ	18	12.90	1.55	14.10
ГОРЬКИЙ	14	11.50	1.10	6.55
ГРОЗНЫЙ	34	29.00	2.20	32.53
ДНЕПРОПЕТРОВСК	21	19.90	1.30	15.00
ДОНЕЦК	22	20.50	1.35	16.43
ДУШАНБЕ	62	50.10	4.05	82.20
ЕРЕВАН	40	33.10	2.50	51.42
ЗАПОРОЖЬЕ	22	20.20	1.50	15.31
ИВАНОВО	12	8.50	1.10	7.55
ИВАНО-ФРАНКОВСК	28	22.20	2.25	30.04
ИЖЕВСК	25	18.30	1.45	22.56
ИРКУТСК	83	55.70	6.50	80.04
ЙОШКАР-ОЛА	18	15.80	1.55	18.25
КАЗАНЬ	19	15.90	1.20	14.45
КАЛИНИНГРАД	26	21.30	1.50	18.29
КАРАГАНДА	52	34.50	4.20	53.50
КАУНАС	22	18.60	2.35	15.00
КЕМЕРОВО	60	39.30	5.05	61.05
КИЕВ	20	17.40	1.20	11.35
КИРОВ	21	18.00	1.40	14.16
КИШИНЕВ	27	24.40	1.50	24.15
КРАСНОДАР	28	24.00	2.25	26.06
КРАСНОЯРСК	68	44.60	5.45	61.05
КРИВОЙ РОГ	24	21.30	3.55	18.14
КУЙБЫШЕВ	22	18.60	1.25	16.23
КУРГАН	37	28.80	3.05	36.39
КУРСК	16	12.40	1.30	7.23
КУСТАНАЙ	39	27.40	2.25	45.00
КУТАИСИ (ЦХАЛТУБО)	35	29.60	2.25	40.50
ЛЕНИНАБАД	58	39.30	5.10	64.19
ЛЕНИНГРАД	18	14.20	1.20	5.59
ЛИПЕЦК	14	11.40	1.05	14.00
ЛЬВОВ	28	23.60	2.25	21.08
МАГНИТОГОРСК	31	27.40	2.30	45.05

4 Look at the chart below. You have to fill in the blanks and work out the costs and the difference in cost and times. The first one is done for you.

	ПÓЕЗДОМ		САМОЛЁТОМ		DIFFERENCES	
	Ценá	Врéмя	Ценá	Врéмя		
Гóрький	11.50	6.55	14	1.10	2p.50к	5hrs.45
Бакý						
Еревáн						
Кíев						
Ленингрáд						
Влади-востóк						

If a plane leaves Moscow at 21.00 hours for Irkutsk what is the local time of arrival?
(*Refer to your time-zone chart in Unit 8.*)

Rivers have played a very significant part in the history of Russian transport. It is partly because of the rivers around it that Moscow became the most important city in Russia. Rivers still play a very important role in the Soviet economy. Because of the volume of their water they may be used for **гидростáнции** *hydro-electric power stations* which are much more easily maintained than atomic power stations and require less man-power. Rivers are also used for goods transport and, where possible, for passenger transport. A **речнóй вокзáл** *river station* is where you will board a **речнóй автóбус** *river bus* or a **кáтер** or **ракéта** which is a large *hydrofoil*. These are common in Leningrad, Kiev and in many other cities where there is a major river.

Лéна, **Обь**, **Енисéй**, Siberian rivers, are used for the transportation of wood and in the western part of Russia canals have been constructed to link the main waterways. The Volga–Don canal is an example of this. There are also great lakes in the Soviet Union, the largest of which is Lake Baikal, which is said to be the deepest lake in the world. One of the electric schemes in the Baikal area **Брáтская ГЭС** is celebrated in poetry by the modern Soviet poet, Yevtushenko.

Writing Russian (iii)

Three letters always have a 'tail' on the front. Make sure that you get the height of the letters right. The letters are *л, м* and *я*. Look at the following examples *дом   красная . лимонад*

write литр ————————————————

write крокодúл ————————————————

write километр ————————————————

write Áнглия ————————————————

Ы is written *ы*   write вы́ход ————————————————

Ю is written *ю* (*Ю*) write меню́ ————————————————

литр

крокодил

километр

Англия

выход

меню

Summary

You should now know most of the expressions you will need to travel around the Soviet Union. Russians love to travel and the size of their country makes it necessary often to undertake long journeys. It is unusual for a Russian to travel long distances by car. He will usually go поездом or самолётом. Most Russians in towns travel автобусом, троллейбусом, трамваем or на метро. They might go on a маршрутное такси or an ordinary такси, but, of course, the latter tends to be rather expensive.

| как проехать | | в | | МГУ
Большой Театр
ГУМ | | ? |

14

What I'd like to do is...

In the last unit you learned about travelling in the Soviet Union. In this one you can find out something about some of the places you might like to visit, and how to say that you want to go there. A useful way of saying what you want is by using the word **бы** with the past tense of **хотéть** — **я хотéл/а бы** *I would like to*...

See Grammar notes (Verbs) page 161

я хотéл бы поéхать (пóездом/самолётом) в Ленингрáд.

я хотéл бы поéхать в Еревáн, etc.

Or, if you're a woman, **я хотéла бы** etc.

Other verbs can be followed in this way by **бы** — **Хорошó бы́ло бы**... *It would be nice to*...

Although the Soviet Union has Moscow as its *capital* (**столи́ца**) the country consists of fifteen republics, each with its own capital. **Ки́ев**, for example, is the capital of the *Ukraine* (**Украи́на**). **Тбили́си** (formerly *Tiflis*) is the capital of *Georgia* (**Гру́зия**). The inhabitants of both cities are conscious of their own nationality and are, of course, not Russians. They also have their own language. Ukrainian resembles Russian in many ways, although the alphabet contains letters not present in Russian. Here is a sample of Ukrainian.

> Раз, два, три, чотири, п'ять —
> Вийшов зайчик погулять.
> Як нам бути, що зробити?
> Треба зайчика зловити.
> Будем знову рахувать:
> Раз, два, три, чотири, п'ять.

You will recognise many of the words from the Russian you already know, and may even be able to work out the main points of the extract. Georgian, an example is shown on the left, is not like Russian at all, and even has its own alphabet.

There are many other languages in the USSR, including Armenian, Estonian, Latvian, Lithuanian, etc. Where Russian is not the first language it is usually taught in schools as a compulsory second language. English is the most widely studied foreign language.

Russian does not vary as much in pronunciation and dialect as English does. 'Standard' Russian is spoken in Moscow and Lenin-

grad, although there are slight differences, and a friendly rivalry exists between the two cities about where the best Russian is spoken.

Leningrad, the second largest city in the Soviet Union, has its own atmosphere. Its origin (1703) is much more recent than Moscow's (1147) and, because it was designed by foreign architects, and in view of its geographical position, it is often considered to be much more 'Western' than other Soviet cities. It has been called a '*window to Europe*' **окно́ в Евро́пу**. The style of its architecture is certainly much more reminiscent of western capitals than you see elsewhere in the Soviet Union. It was, of course, the capital of Russia from the time of Peter the Great until March 1918. In 1914 its name was changed from St. Petersburg to Petrograd and it became Leningrad after the death of Lenin in 1924.

Comprehension Here are some notes in Russian about some of the main cities of the Soviet Union. Each set of notes is followed by two questions in English.

Гла́вные города́ Сове́тского Сою́за
Москва́

about
are situated

stands
for example
call

* и т.д.: и так далее (and so on; etc.)

Столи́ца СССР с 1918ого го́да. В Москве́ живёт **о́коло** десяти́ миллио́нов челове́к. В це́нтре го́рода **нахо́дятся** Кремль, Кра́сная пло́щадь и гла́вная у́лица — у́лица Го́рького. Москва́ **стои́т** на Москва́-реке́. На проспе́кте Кали́нина нахо́дятся но́вые магази́ны, **наприме́р** «Мело́дия», «Дом кни́ги» и т.д.,* — Москвичи́ **называ́ют** э́тот райо́н Но́вый Арба́т.

1 How many people live in Moscow?_____

2 Where are the new shops in Moscow?_____

Ленинград

В Ленингра́де мно́го краси́вых **зда́ний**, музе́ев, собо́ров. Ули́цы в Ленингра́де **прямы́е** и **широ́кие**. Гла́вная у́лица — Не́вский проспе́кт. В Ленингра́де, кото́рый называ́лся до револю́ции Петербу́ргом, нахо́дится Эрмита́ж, где мо́жно уви́деть уника́льные колле́кции рабо́т **за́падных** и ру́сских **худо́жников**. Гла́вная река́ — Нева́. В Ленингра́де 365 **мосто́в** и мно́го кана́лов. Ленингра́д — «**Се́верная** Вене́ция» Росси́и.

1 What was Leningrad called before the Revolution?_____
2 Why was it called the 'Northern Venice'?_____

Ки́ев

Столи́ца Украи́ны. Стои́т на реке́ Днепр. Ки́ев краси́вый, **зелёный** го́род с па́рками и **сада́ми**. На Днепре́ в Ки́еве есть речно́й вокза́л. **Отту́да** мо́жно пое́хать на ка́тере на пляж. В Ки́еве, как и в Москве́ и в Ленингра́де, есть метро́. Гла́вная у́лица называ́ется Креща́тик.

1 What's the name of the river?_____
2 What's the name of the main street?_____

Тбили́си

(**ра́ньше** Тифли́с) Столи́ца Гру́зии. О́чень ста́рый го́род на Кавка́зе. Он стои́т на реке́ Куре́ и архитекту́ра в нём кавка́зская. **Знамени́тый** поэ́т Гру́зии — Шота́ Руставе́ли. Гла́вная у́лица — проспе́кт Руставе́ли. В музе́е — интере́сные **карти́ны** Ни́ко Пиросманашви́ли (Пиросма́ни).

1 Which mountains are near Tbilisi? _____
2 What's the name of a famous Georgian artist?_____

Ри́га

Столи́ца Латви́йской Сове́тской Социалисти́ческой Респу́блики (Ла́твии) на се́веро-за́паде Сове́тского Сою́за. Ри́га о́чень большо́й порт на Балти́йском мо́ре. Там живёт 740 ты́сяч челове́к. Ста́рая Ри́га о́чень интере́сня.

1 Of which republic is Riga the capital?_____
2 Which part of Riga is interesting?_____

Ташке́нт

Столи́ца Узбекиста́на, респу́блики в Сре́дней А́зии. Там есть тексти́льные фа́брики. В Ташке́нте живёт 1,5м челове́к. Самарка́нд и Бухара́ то́же нахо́дятся в Узбекиста́не.

1 What sort of factories are in Tashkent?_____
2 What's the population? _____

See Grammar notes (Adjectives) page 158

You will notice that many of these words are adjectives, describing words. The endings of these words change when they are used. You have already come across **Кра́сная** пло́щадь and a number of other adjectives; **зелёный** is another colour. **Бе́лый** *white* as in **Белору́ссия** *White Russia*, **бе́лые но́чи** *White Nights* and **чёрный** (**Очи чёрные** — *Black Eyes*, the song), **Чёрное мо́ре** *Black Sea* are two more. The Russians distinguish between *light blue* **голубо́й** and *deep blue* **си́ний**. Other adjectives you might find useful are **чуде́сный** *wonderful*, **ужа́сный** *terrible*, and **высо́кий** *high*.

Points of the compass

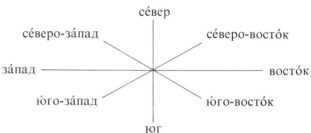

1 Complete the following sentences, saying which direction (North, South, etc.) the place is in.

1   Тбили́си нахо́дится на _____ Сове́тского Сою́за.

2   Ри́га нахо́дится на _____ Сове́тского Сою́за.

3   Владивосто́к нахо́дится на _____ Сове́тского Сою́за.

4   Ташке́нт нахо́дится на _____ _____ Сове́тского Сою́за.

5   Ленингра́д нахо́дится на _____ _____ Росси́и.

6   Манче́стер нахо́дится на _____ А́нглии.

2 Here is an essay written by a schoolgirl in Moscow. Watch for the past tenses, and for examples of **бы** (see beginning of unit).

Города́, в кото́рых я была́.

В 1971 году́ мы жи́ли в Ленингра́де. Па́па там рабо́тал в Университе́те. Ленингра́д о́чень краси́вый го́род. Па́па е́здил ка́ждый день на тролле́йбусе в Университе́т. Мне нра́вилось гуля́ть но Не́вскому проспе́кту, где мы с ма́мой смотре́ли на **витри́ны** магази́нов. В 1973 па́па чита́л ле́кцию на конфере́нции в Ки́евском Университе́те, и мы с ма́мой то́же е́здили туда́. Там бы́ло о́чень интере́сно. Мы е́хали ночны́м по́ездом. Гости́ница в Ки́еве была́ краси́вая и в

windows

центре го́рода. Я ра́ньше не зна́ла, что в Ки́еве есть метро́. В Ки́еве мы с ма́мой гуля́ли в па́рке у Днепра́, а ве́чером мы смотре́ли в кино́ украи́нские фи́льмы.

Я хоте́ла бы пое́хать в Тбили́си. В 1980 году́ там бу́дет конфере́нция. Па́па хоте́л бы чита́ть там ле́кцию. Я бы то́же хоте́ла туда́ пое́хать. Бы́ло бы хорошо́ увидеть высо́кие *mountains* **го́ры** на Кавка́зе.

1	Where did the girl's father work?
2	What did the girl like to do?
3	What was the occasion of their visit?
4	How did they travel?
5	What surprised her about Kiev?
6	What did they do in Kiev?
7	Where else would the girl like to go?

3 Look at the first example below, which is done for you, and see if you can answer the other questions in a similar way. Print or write your answers in the spaces provided.

1 **Q** Ни́на бу́дет в теа́тре сего́дня ве́чером?

   A Она́ хоте́ла бы пойти́, но теа́тр сего́дня закры́т.

2 **Q** Бори́с бу́дет в рестора́не сего́дня ве́чером?

   A _____

3 **Q** А́нна и Ка́тя бу́дут в библиоте́ке сего́дня ве́чером?

   A _____

4 **Q** Бори́с бу́дет в кино́ сего́дня ве́чером?

   A _____

Writing Russian (iv)

Some of the capital letters are written with a flourish, and give written Russian a much more ornate appearance than written English. Try writing all the examples given below with large letters at the beginning

Ф is written _ф_ (_Ф_)   write Фо́то _____

Ч is written _ч_ (_Ч_)   write Чай _____

write Че́хов _____

ь is written _ь_   write Февра́ль _____

write Кре́мль _____

Б is written _б_ _Б_   write Грибы́ _____

write Бюро́ _____

write Бланк _____

Э is written _э_ _Э_   write Экску́рсия _____

Summary

You have learned another way to ask for things (**хоте́л бы**) and have seen some of the words that you will come across in connection with towns. You have also seen some more adjectives and acquainted yourself with the points of the compass.

я хоте́л(а) бы	пое́хать в Ленингра́д
	пойти́ в кино́

бы́ло бы хорошо́	пойти́ в теа́тр
	пое́хать в Тбили́си

_Фо́то_

Чай

Че́хов

_Ро́ль_

Кре́мль

Грибы́

Бюро́

Бланк

Экску́рсия

112

15 | Revision

In Units 11–14 we looked at ways of saying when things happened. We also showed you a little of Russian history. In this unit we are going to revise some of these points and provide you with a series of exercises you can use to test your present grasp of the language. First of all, however, we would like you to add two items to your vocabulary. **Век** means century, so *in the nineteenth century* is **в девятнáдцатом вéке**. The word for *thousand* is **тысяча**, and the way to say *in 1861* is **в тысяча восемьсот шестьдесят первом году.**

1 ◗ See if you can work out the following dates. The first one is done for you. Write the figure in the space provided.

1	В тысяча двести двáдцать трéтьем годý	в 1223г.
2	В тысяча триста двáдцать шестóм годý	
3	В тысяча шестьсóт пятом годý	
4	В тысяча семьсóт трéтьем годý	
5	В тысяча восемьсóт шестьдесят пéрвом годý	
6	В тысяча девятьсóт пятьдесят трéтьем годý	

2 ◗ All the above dates refer to the list in unit 12. Now look at the list and say what happened. **Что случилось?** Answer in Russian.

1 _____

2 _____

3 _____

4 _____

5 _____

6 _____

3 ■ Now here are three jumbled lists. Again, referring to the list of dates in unit 12, take one item from the list on the left, one from the centre and one from the third to form a complete sentence. Do this by joining the boxes together.

В 1227г.	Пётр Вели́кий	пе́рвая мирова́я война́
В 1914г.	ко́нчилась	Екатери́на II
В 1697г.	у́мер	тата́рское и́го
В 1945г.	начала́сь	Чинги́з-хан
В 1480г.	умерла́	пое́хал в Голла́ндию
В 1796г.	ко́нчилось	втора́я мирова́я война́

Here is a letter from a student in Moscow University to his friend in Leningrad. Some of the words have been missed out. First of all look through the letter and see if you can decide what kind of words are missing. Then go on to the exercises below.

Москва́, четве́рг 20ого сентября́ 1979

Дорого́й Бо́ря,
Вот я и в Моско́вском Университе́те. Мы _____1____ ле́кции
ago   и семина́ры две неде́ли **наза́д**. На́шего профе́ссора по фи́зике
_____2____ Бори́сов, Ива́н Никола́евич. _____3____, что он
из Ки́ева. Вчера́ он _____4____ о́чень интере́сную ле́кцию о
ко́смосе. По́сле ле́кции мы _____5____ в студе́нческой столо́-
вой, а пото́м _____6____ телеви́зор. Америка́нский пиани́ст
_____7____ конце́рт Чайко́вского. За́втра мы бу́дем _____8____
в лаборато́рии, а ве́чером бу́дем _____9____ в библиоте́ке.
Мне ну́жно _____10____ о́чень мно́го рабо́тать, но я могу́
занима́ться и спо́ртом. Здесь мы _____11____ в воллейбо́л,
хокке́й, в насто́льный те́ннис и т.д.

Приве́т ма́ме и па́пе,
Ва́ня.

P.S. Пиши́ скоре́е, прошу́ тебя́!

4 Some of the verbs have been missed out from the passage above. They are listed below. Put the number of the space where they belong in the box provided, and then answer, in Russian, the questions below. Give short answers.

смотре́ли	⬜	игра́ем	⬜
зову́т	⬜	бу́дет	⬜
чита́л	⬜	на́чали	⬜
у́жинали	⬜	игра́л	⬜
чита́ть	⬜	говоря́т	⬜
рабо́тать	⬜		

5

course

1	Како́го числа́ на́чался **курс**?
2	Как зову́т профе́ссора?
3	В како́й день профе́ссор чита́л ле́кцию?
4	Како́го числа́ Ва́ня бу́дет в лаборато́рии?

country

5	Из како́й **страны́** пиани́ст? Он из

6 You are due to go from Leningrad to Moscow by plane. You discover that Pulkovo airport in Leningrad is closed, and will not be open for another four days. You have to send a telegram to a friend telling him that you will be coming by train and when you will be in Moscow (10.00 a.m. on Wednesday, 8th August). Make up the telegram. Use the form on page 120.

7 ■ Here are some instructions in a hotel in Riga for using the telephone.

	1 Телефо́н-автома́т рабо́тает от двухкопе́ечной моне́ты.
free	2 Из но́мера гости́ницы в преде́лах го́рода мо́жно позвони́ть **беспла́тно**.
if, dial	3 **Е́сли** вы хоти́те звони́ть в го́род, **набери́те** «0», пото́м ну́жный но́мер телефо́на.
in order to	4 **Что́бы** звони́ть из го́рода в гости́ницу, набери́те 210, пото́м но́мер ну́жной вам ко́мнаты.

1   How much does it cost to telephone from a booth? _____

2   Which telephone calls are free? _____

3   What do you have to do to dial a town number? _____
   _____

4   If you dial 210662, which room in the hotel would you get? ____

In Moscow telephone numbers consist of seven figures and if you are in a hotel (e.g. Росси́я), they have a prefix, e.g. 225, followed by your room number (427) and then the floor you're on (e.g. 6). In this case your number is 225-42-76. Russians always group the numbers in this way. If you add the international code for Moscow and you have a number that can be dialled directly, it is possible to receive international dialled calls directly into your room. If you want to phone out, you normally have to order a call well in advance.

8 ■ Look at the ice-hockey league table and results below, and then answer the questions in Russian. Put your answers in the spaces provided.

ВЫСШАЯ ЛИГА

Положение на 24 сентября

* ЦСКА — «Салават Юлаев» — 7:1 (1:0, 3:0, 3:1)
* «Динамо» Р — «Спартак» — 2:3 (2:1, 0:1, 0:1)
* «Автомобилист» — «Динамо» М — 1:9 (1:3, 0:4, 0:2)
* СКА — «Химик» — 1:5 (0:2, 1:3, 0:0)
* «Сокол» — «Трактор» — 1:4 (1:0, 0:4, 0:0)

	И	В	Н	П	Голы	Очки
1. ЦСКА	6	6	0	0	41 — 16	12 — 0
2. «Трактор»	6	5	1	0	27 — 14	11 — 1
3. «Динамо» М	6	4	1	1	42 — 19	9 — 3
4. «Химик»	6	3	1	2	28 — 21	7 — 5
5. «Крылья Советов»	6	3	1	2	21 — 17	7 — 5
6. «Спартак»	6	3	1	2	22 — 21	7 — 5
7. «Торпедо»	6	3	0	3	22 — 27	6 — 6
8. «Динамо» Р	6	2	0	4	16 — 19	4 — 8
9. «Салават Юлаев»	6	2	0	4	18 — 31	4 — 8
10. «Сокол»	6	1	0	5	18 — 27	2 — 10
11. СКА	6	1	0	5	22 — 39	2 — 10
12. «Автомобилист»	6	0	1	5	12 — 38	1 — 11

НА СЧЕТУ БОМБАРДИРОВ

В. БЕЛОУСОВ
«Трактор» — 12(8+4)

П. ПРИРОДИН
«Динамо» (М) — 11(4+7)

А. ГОЛИКОВ
«Динамо» (М) — 10(7+3)

В. ПЕТРОВ
ЦСКА — 10(5+5)

1 Who was playing against Moscow Dynamo?
2 What was the result of the match between SKA and Khimik?
3 Who is first in the league?
4 Who has nine points (Очки)?
5 How many points has Spartak?
6 Who is in twelfth place?
7 Who is the leading scorer (бомбардир)?

Sport plays an important part in Soviet education and children are encouraged to take part in it in their spare time. The education of a Soviet child takes a fairly set pattern. Although there are different kinds of schools: *boarding schools* **интернаты**, *secondary schools* **средние школы** and special schools of various kinds, including schools where some subjects are taught in English, the overall system is uniform. A child may go to a *nursery* **ясли**, then a *kindergarten* **детский сад** and at seven he starts school. Most of the schools are ten-year schools and there are various 'milestones' in a school career. If a pupil is not doing well in school, he may be left behind to repeat a year. Compulsory education starts at seven. On the next page is the history of the education of a typical Soviet child.

Вот Ми́ша. Тепе́рь ему́ три го́да, и он хо́дит в де́тский сад.	Тепе́рь ему́ семь лет, и он хо́дит в шко́лу.	Он в пе́рвом кла́ссе. Он октябрёнок.	Тепе́рь ему́ де́сять лет, и он у́чится в четвёртом кла́ссе.
Он пионе́р.	Ми́ша хорошо́ у́чится и сдаёт все экза́мены на отли́чно, на пять.	В седьмо́м кла́ссе он стано́вится комсомо́льцем.	Тепе́рь ему́ два́дцать лет. Он студе́нт Моско́вского Университе́та.

Экза́мены. These may be written or oral. In the oral examinations students are given a *choice of cards* **экзаменацио́нные биле́ты** with questions written on them, and then given time to prepare the answers. They are then marked on a 5-point scale.

5 = **отли́чно** *excellent*
4 = **хорошо́** *good*
3 = **удовлетвори́тельно** *satisfactory*
2 = **неудовлетвори́тельно** *unsatisfactory* (*fail*)
1 = **о́чень пло́хо** *very poor*

It is almost unheard of for anyone to get 1. 'Fail' is usually 2.

In diploma examinations (from degree level upwards) candidates have to 'defend' their diploma. This means that having done a piece of written work they have to stand up in front of an audience and summarise the main arguments. The audience may then ask questions before the external *examiners* (**оппоне́нты**), give their opinions and recommend marks, again on a five-point scale. If a student decides to go on to postgraduate work, he can become a **кандида́т** by passing oral exams as well as writing a dissertation. The final stage is **до́ктор нау́к**, and many Russians take this degree late in life. The most famous academics become members of the *Academy of Sciences* **Акаде́мия Нау́к**. This membership is much sought after, as it carries many privileges.

Слов	Плата			МИНИСТЕРСТВО СВЯЗИ СССР	ПЕРЕДАЧА
	руб.	коп.			

ТЕЛЕГРАММА

Из _____

№ _____

_____ сл. _____ го _____ час. _____ мин.

Итого

Принял _____

ПЕРЕДАЧА

_____ го _____ час. _____ мин.

№ связи _____

Передал: _____

Служебн. отметки

Категория и отметки особого вида: _____

Куда, кому _____

_____

_____

_____

_____

_____

_____

Фамилия отправителя и его адрес (в счет слов не входят, не оплачиваются и по телеграфу не передаются).

Тип «Ставр. правда», 1971 г. 911 13.930.000

В начале телеграммы перед текстом пишется категория (срочная), особый вид (уведомление телеграфом, вручить лично, ответ и др.), куда, кому.

Writing Russian (v)

The most ornate of the letters have been saved till the end. Write all the words with a capital letter.

Ж is written *Ж (Ж)*   write Этáж_____

write Мóжно_____

Ш is written *ш (Ш)*   write Хорошó_____

Щ is written *щ (Щ)*   write Ещё_____

Ц is written *ц (Ц)*   write Цирк_____

write Щи_____

write Жéнщина_____

Most Russians write with a forward slope, and exercise books in schools have lines to indicate where the slope should be (//////// etc.). Children are also encouraged to be right-handed in writing.

Этáж
Мóжно
Хорошó
Ещё
Цирк
Щи
Жéнщина

120

16 | Expressing opinions

Russians pride themselves on their *hospitality* **гостеприи́мство**. If they get a chance they will enjoy comparing things in the Soviet Union with things in the West and sometimes this can lead to discussions of opinions, preferences, and so on. In this unit you will learn some of the words and phrases you will need for such discussions. Look at the following dialogue. It's also on your recording. A Muscovite is sitting next to a couple of British girls in a restaurant. He tries to engage them in conversation.

— Извини́те, отку́да вы?
— Из Великобрита́нии!
— Вы отли́чно говори́те по-ру́сски.
— Спаси́бо.
— Вы студе́нтки?
— Да.
— Я то́же студе́нт. Прости́те, меня́ зову́т Ива́н Бори́сович. Фами́лия Бело́в.
— Я А́нна, а э́то Мэ́ри.
— О́чень прия́тно. Вы из Ло́ндона?
— Нет, из Эдинбу́рга.
— Интере́сно. Ну и как дела́ у вас в А́нглии?
— Мы не из А́нглии, а из Шотла́ндии.

the same — Для нас в СССР э́то **то же са́мое**.

121

agreed	— А я не **согласна**.
that is	— Скажите, у вас в Áнглии — **то-есть**, в Шотландии, женщины любят виски?
	— Нет, я виски не люблю.
	— А вот у вас водка. Знаете, у нас в СССР женщины любят вино, шампанское, пиво, коктейли даже, может быть, и коньяк, а водку — нет, никогда.
matter of taste, more than	— Это **дело вкуса**. Водка мне **больше** нравится, **чем** виски.
in my opinion	— Нет, **по-моему** это не дело вкуса. Дело в том, что у нас женщины **меньше** пьют, **чем** у вас.
less than	
	— Может быть.
of course	— **Конечно.** А скажите, если вы из Шотландии, почему вы не в шотландской **юбке**? Говорят, что там даже мужчины **носят** юбки. Это правда?
skirt, wear	
	— Да что вы говорите! Это не так! В Шотландии солдаты носят юбки. И потом это национальный костюм. **Иногда** по праздникам мужчины носят юбки. Вот и всё!
sometimes	
policemen	— А **милиционеры**?
	— Извините, но уже шесть часов. У нас билеты в театр.
play	— **Пьеса** начинается в семь часов.
	— В какой театр вы идёте? В Большой?
	— На Таганку.
spare	— Ой-ой-ой, как хорошо! У вас нет **лишнего** билета!
unfortunately	— **К сожалению**, нет. До свидания.
	— До свидания. Всего доброго. Вы будете здесь завтра вечером?
	— Я думаю, нет.

1 📖 📺 Answer the questions in English

1 Where are the British girls from?_____

2 What do Soviet women like to drink?_____

_____

3 Why does the Russian student think it's not a matter of taste?

_____

4 Why is the Soviet student surprised at the way the girls dress?

_____

5 What do they tell him about this?_____

6 Where are the girls going?_____

The preceding dialogue is fortunately not typical of exchanges between British tourists and Soviet citizens, but it does serve to illustrate some useful expressions. **Согла́сен** *agreed* — **я согла́сен** *I agree*, **я/она́ согла́сна, мы/вы/они́ согла́сны**. In the dialogue the girl disagrees **я не согла́сна**.

Зна́ете *you know* is used as a 'filler'. If you listen to some Russians speaking English, you will hear them make too frequent use of such expressions as '*you know...*', '*it seems to me...*' **мне ка́жется**, '*I think*' **я ду́маю**, *in my opinion* **по-мо́ему**. This is because Russians use these expressions frequently in their own language, and transfer them when speaking English.

See Grammar notes (Comparatives) page 159

You have come across the expressions **мне нра́вится** *I like* and **мне о́чень нра́вится** *I very much like*. Here you have **мне бо́льше** нра́вится (*I like more*, e.g. *I prefer*). The opposite of this is **мне ме́ньше** нра́вится (*I like less*). These forms are called 'comparatives'. Other common comparatives are **лу́чше** *better* and **ху́же** *worse*.

2 Here is an exercise to illustrate comparatives. You have to supply the missing word and state the nationality of the person making the statement. The first one is done for you.

1 — У вас в А́нглии библиоте́ки лу́чше, чем в Москве́?
   — Нет, ху́же (англича́нин)

2 — Скажи́те, у вас в Нью-йо́рке бо́льше авто́бусов, чем в Москве́?
   — Нет, _____ (   )

3 — Скажи́те, у вас в СССР ме́ньше пьют, чем в Япо́нии?
   — Нет, _____ (   )

4 — Как вам ка́жется, у вас в Шотла́ндии ме́ньше пьют ви́ски, чем в Аме́рике?

   — Нет, _____ (   )

Another way of saying **мне бо́льше нра́вится** is **я предпочита́ю** *I prefer* or **я предпочита́л/а бы** *I should prefer*. Look at the following exercise.

3 ■ Husbands and wives do not always agree, even in the Soviet Union! In the following exchanges the wife chooses the opposite to her husband. See if you can complete her sentences. Sometimes there is a word missing in the middle. You should be able to guess it from the context. The first one is done for you.

1 Муж — Вот, в меню́ есть бифштéксы и ры́ба.
Мне, пожáлуйста, бифштéкс.

Женá — Я предпочитáю ры́бу.

2 М. — Мóжно поéхать и́ли автóбусом и́ли троллéйбусом.
Поéдем автóбусом!

Ж. — Нет, лýчше _____ _____ .

3 М. — Фильм идёт в воскресéнье и в четвéрг. Пойдём в воскресéнье.

Ж. — А я предпочитáла бы _____ __ _____ .

4 М. — Сегóдня интерéсная прогрáмма по телеви́зору, я не хочý идти́ в теáтр.

Ж. — А я _____ бы _____ в теáтр.

5 М. — Что ты предпочитáешь — óперу и́ли балéт? Я хотéл бы послýшать óперу.

Ж. — А я предпочитáю _____ .

4 It's a matter of taste. Here are some incomplete statements about various nationalities and places. You have to choose the correct alternative from the column on the left and place its number in the box to complete the sentence on the right. Do the most likely ones first.

1	В Шотла́ндии	☐	бо́льше лю́бят вино́, чем пи́во
2	Во Фра́нции	☐	бо́льше икры́, чем в Ита́лии
3	Англича́не	☐	ме́ньше коммунистов, чем в Кита́е
4	В Япо́нии	☐	предпочита́ют жить в А́нглии
5	Америка́нцы	☐	бо́льше лю́бят ви́ски, чем во́дку
6	В СССР	☐	о́чень лю́бят бейсбо́л

Summary

You should now be able to recognise some of the ways in which Russians agree and disagree with one another. Because of the differences between British and Soviet societies, Russians will often want to know about what is *better* **лу́чше** and what is *worse* **ху́же**, what we have *more of* **бо́льше** and what we have *less of* **ме́ньше**. They will also want to know your opinion **Как вам ка́жется…?** *How does it seem to you…?* or **Как по-ва́шему…?** You should now be equipped to reply in simple terms to all of these.

17

Congratulations!

It is not always easy to find exact English equivalents for Russian expressions, and this is particularly true of Russian greetings. Perhaps the most common of these is '**здравствуйте**', which is related to the word **здоровье** *health* and literally means 'be well!' It is used as we would use 'Hello' as is, more informally, '**привет**!' '*How are you?* would be '**Как вы поживаете?**' or, less formally, '**Как живёшь?**' or '**Как дела?**' *How are things?*, to which the reply might be '**Хорошо**, а вы/ты?' or '**ничего**' (o.k.).

Two expressions you will come across are '**всего хорошего**' *all the best* and '**спокойной ночи**' *good night*. In Russia, as in Germany or France, it is normal to wish someone '*good appetite*' '**приятного аппетита**'. The reply in Russian would be simply '**спасибо**'. In the above expressions the endings of the words change, but they do not change in such expressions as '**доброе утро**' *good morning*, '**добрый вечер**' *good evening* and '**добрый день**' *good day*.

Another greeting expression that you will see is **С днём рождения**!* *Happy Birthday!* or **С праздником!** *Happy feast day!* These are the sort of expressions that might appear on greetings cards. Russians congratulate one another by using the word **поздравляю** (lit. *I congratulate*). **Желаю вам всего хорошего** (*I wish you all the best*).

* Russians also celebrate 'name days'. These were originally religious feast days of their patron saints.

Grammar notes (*Genitive*) page 155

Here are some expressions you might see or hear. You will have met some of them before in the course.

Привет	— Greetings, regards
Передайте ему горячий привет	— Give him my warmest regards
С приветом	— Regards (at the end of a letter)
Целую и обнимаю	— I kiss and embrace you
С новым годом	— Happy New Year
Поздравляю	— Congratulations
Будьте здоровы	— Keep well
Всего хорошего/доброго	— All the best

1 ◗Here is another letter. This time we have missed out, not the verbs, but the expressions of greeting. See if you can fill in the gaps using expressions you have seen so far in this unit. Write your answers in the spaces provided. Pay attention to the dates when you fill in the first two items.

1ое января, 1980

Дорогóй Сáша!

Я всегдá дýмаю о тебé в э́то врéмя гóда! Ты, как и я, роди-

лáсь 2ого января. С ＿＿＿＿＿＿＿ ＿＿＿＿＿＿＿ и с

＿＿＿＿＿＿＿ ＿＿＿＿＿＿＿! Как твой муж? Передáй

ему ＿＿＿＿＿＿＿ ＿＿＿＿＿＿＿. Мúла мне сказáла,

что твой сын сдал экзáмены в прóшлом годý. ＿＿＿＿＿＿!

Он дéлает большúе успéхи! У меня́ есть хорóшие нóвости.

Муж получúл рабóту в Москвé. Мы с тобóй чáсто бýдем

встречáться, как и рáньше.

＿＿＿＿＿＿＿-ую и ＿＿＿＿＿＿＿-аю

＿＿＿＿＿＿＿ ＿＿＿＿＿＿＿

Тáня　127

One of the features of streets everywhere in the Soviet Union is the presence of slogans. You have come across Ми́ру мир — Peace to the World. Others you might see are:

Пролета́рии всех стран, соединя́йтесь!
(lit. Proletariats of all countries, unite!)

Ле́нин с на́ми!
Lenin is with us!

Побе́да Социали́зму!
Victory for Socialism!

Да здра́вствует но́вая Конститу́ция!
Long live the new constitution!

Сла́ва труду́!
Glory to Labour!

These often appear on hoardings or above buildings. *Congresses of the Party* **Съе́зды Па́ртии** are also commemorated as important events.

Besides *the first of May* **Первома́й**, the Russians have a number of other *holidays* **пра́здники**. The main winter holiday is the *New Year* **Но́вый год**, which tends to last for a week or ten days. The other public holidays are International Women's Day on 8th March, 1st May and 2nd May, Victory Day on 9th May, the Anniversary of the October Revolution on 7th and 8th November and Constitution Day on 7th October. If you are going on business to the Soviet Union, try to avoid these dates: you may not get much work done!

8ᵒᵉ ма́рта   — Междунаро́дный же́нский день
9ᵒᵉ ма́я   — День побе́ды
7ᵒᵉ октября́   — День конститу́ции СССР
7ᵒᵉ и 8ᵒᵉ   — Пра́здник Октября́. Годовщи́на
ноября́   Социалисти́ческой Револю́ции.

(между — *inter-* — народ — *nation* — ный — *-al* ^(here))
(год — *year* — годовщи́на *anniversary*)

The Gregorian calendar, adopted in England in 1752, was not introduced in Russia until 1918, i.e. after the Revolution. This is why the October Revolution has its anniversary in November and why many Orthodox Russians celebrate Christmas on January 7th. Peter the Great changed the Orthodox New Year's Day from September to January. This caused an outcry. 'The world,' it was explained 'could not have been created in January, as the new calendar seemed to indicate, because apples are not ripe at that season, and consequently Eve could not have been tempted in the way described!'*

* D. Mackenzie Wallace, 'Russia', 1877.

Победа means 'victory'. A common slogan is Коммунизм победит. Победить (to be victorious) is the usual word used to indicate a sporting victory.

2 ◼ Look at the passage below and see if you can answer the questions that follow it. Don't worry if you don't understand all the words. The key roots are given in the margin. Look at these roots and make your best guess at the information in the passage.

очко́ = point
ю́н/ый = young
пе́рв/ый = first
ша́хматы = chess
го́нки = race
велосипе́д = bicycle

старты и финиши

Москвич Сергей Долматов, набрав 10,5 очка, вышел победителем юношеского первенства мира по шахматам, завершившегося в австрийском городе Граце. На втором месте — теперь уже экс-чемпион мира его земляк Артур Юсупов, отставший от Долматова на 0,5 очка. Третье место занял датчанин Енс Фриз-Нильсен.

Победой советских спортсменов закончилась 16-я велогонка «Тур де Л′авенир» по дорогам Франции. Победителем состязаний (1590 км) стал Сергей Сухорученков из Куйбышева — 42 часа 26 мин. 28 сек. Следующие три места заняли также наши спортсмены — Рамазан Галялетдинов из Куйбышева, ленинградец Сергей Морозов и победитель велогонки Мира-78 Александр Аверин из Куйбышева.

1 What did Dolmatov win?

2 Where did it take place?

3 What can you learn about Yusupov?

4 What was the surname of the man who came third?

5 Where did the bicycle race take place?

6 Who won the bicycle race and what was his time?

7 Who were the runners-up and which towns did they come from?

КРОССВО́РД

Across

1 This is a пра́здник for Russians
7 Kind or breed (from роди́ться)*
10 You find this in Крокоди́л
11 But
13 Daddy
14 Same as 11
15 Greetings!
17 Мы вчера́ бы́ли _____ концёрте.
18 С Но́вым _____ .
19 Толсто́й жил в девятна́дцатом _____ .
20 Central Committee (abbrev.)
21 Он пришёл к _____ пе́рвым и стал победи́телем.
26 A female Tatar
27 Often figures on Soviet slogans
29 Well now
30 У Ма́ши _____ и до́чка
31 Hall — comes after мю́зик
32 Пётр Вели́кий, наприме́р (for example)
33 I go
34 Пе́рвый _____ ; for Soviet schoolchildren
37 Оди́н век = _____ лет
39 Baghdad had one of these*
42 North Pole (initials)
44 The first is a celebration
45 Столи́ца Япо́нии*
46 Old name for Russia
47 Paradise*
49 Fast run or swim
50 Большо́й _____ наприме́р
51 House of Culture (initials)
52 This also has its own day
55 You'd celebrate if you won this!
58 Компози́тор из Герма́нии. И.С. _____ *
60 _____ фа́брике есть клуб
61 This is what players try to score
62 В _____ -па́рке жира́ф и тигр
63 Russia does not belong to this organisation of the North Atlantic*
64 In autumn
65 Academy of Sciences (initials)
66 Short girl's name

Down

1 Russian name for Copernicus*
2 _____ is a fair description for a citizen of the USSR
3 Track*
4 Hymn sung by socialists
5 Sound of musical instrument
6 Inhabitant of 45 across
7 О́чень _____ is what you say to someone when you meet
8 It
9 Building or house
10 Little Ю́рий or French mountain range
12 Bed-time drink for some
13 Along
16 A terrible Russian king
20 20 across in a different direction
21 Underground station 3 stops West after Ки́евская. (Map page 80)
22 Someone who does иллюстра́ции
23 Д ___ ___ ___ МО: Football team
24 Wide
25 У нас в Москве́ мно́го теа́тров, а как _____ вас в А́нглии?
26 Вы идёте в парк? Я то́же иду
28 Большо́й го́род в Шта́тах
35 Starts the action for 49 across
36 35 and 49 are both at this point
37 Хокке́й популя́рный _____ в Сове́тском Сою́зе.
38 So!
40 If you miss the train at 21, you'll still be here
41 У нас лу́чше? Нет, наоборо́т _____ !
43 В про́шлом году́ в на́шем университе́те была́ больша́я _____ сове́тских студе́нтов
44 Rubbish*
48 Name of an old street in Moscow. There is a Metro station at the end of it
51 Another word for число́ (date)
53 Encore
54 River which quietly flows
56 UNO (initials). United = объединённых
57 They
59 Red army has one
62 In exchange for or in favour of

130

* Words marked thus are new. Many of them you will be able to guess. Most of them will appear when you solve associated clues.

18

Expressing feelings

This unit is about two aspects of feelings — those to do with health and those to do with emotions. First of all, questions of health (здоро́вье) and how to cope if you fall ill in the USSR.

If you are unfortunate enough to fall ill during a visit to the Soviet Union, help will usually be very prompt and always completely free of charge. Here's what to do: ring the *service bureau* **бюро́ обслу́живания** in your hotel and tell them. They will arrange for a doctor to come to your room. Many of the large hotels have a **Медпу́нкт**, where qualified people work permanently, so treatment can often be obtained on the spot.

Here is a dialogue that might occur in such a situation. **Т** = Тури́ст, **Деж** = Дежу́рная *floor superintendent*, **Б.о.** = Бюро́ обслу́живания and **В** = Врач *doctor*. The dialogue is split into sections with stage directions between each section. It is also on your recording.

Тури́ст набира́ет но́мер

Па́уза.

Бюро́ обслу́живания: Бюро́ обслу́живания.

Тури́ст: Скажи́те, пожа́луйста, что мне де́лать? Мне ка́жется, я

ill
give

заболе́л.

Б.о. Я **даю́** вам Медпу́нкт.

Па́уза.

Медпу́нкт: Медпу́нкт.

high
sore throat
understood
head
half an hour
cold

Т: Я говорю́ из но́мера 345. Мне ка́жется, у меня́ **высо́кая** температу́ра. И о́чень **боли́т го́рло.**

М: Так. **Поня́тно.** Что ещё?

Т: Голова́ то́же боли́т, но не о́чень.

М: Так. Врач бу́дет у вас че́рез **полчаса́.** Я ду́маю, что э́то **просту́да.** Закажи́те че́рез дежу́рную чай с лимо́ном. Э́то иногда́ о́чень помога́ет.

Т: Спаси́бо.

131

Через пять минут.

Дежу́рная: (вхо́дит) Здра́вствуйте. Вот вам чай с лимо́ном.

Т: Спаси́бо.

Деж: Заболе́ли, да? Врач сейча́с бу́дет. Пе́йте чай. Е́сли хоти́те что-нибу́дь ещё, позвони́те.

Т: Спаси́бо большо́е.

Че́рез 20 мину́т.

Вра́ч: (вхо́дит) Мо́жно?

Т: Пожа́луйста, входи́те.

В: Здра́вствуйте. Я уже́ зна́ю, что у вас боли́т го́рло.

Т: И голова́.

В: А как аппети́т?

at all **Т:** Аппети́та **совсе́м** нет.

В: Покажи́те, пожа́луйста, го́рло. Скажи́те «А-а-а».

Т: «А-а-а».

В: Гм. Посмо́трим, кака́я у вас температу́ра. Вот термо́метр.

Па́уза.

В: Да, у вас есть температу́ра, но не о́чень высо́кая.

flu **Т:** Это **грипп**, до́ктор?

В: Нет, просту́да. Я вам вы́пишу реце́пт. Принима́йте э́ти табле́тки три ра́за в день. Вы должны́ лежа́ть, отдыха́ть. За́втра я бу́ду у вас. Е́сли вам бу́дет ху́же, позвони́те опя́ть в медпу́нкт.

1 📖 🔲 Answer the following questions:

1	What are the tourist's symptoms?
2	What does the person in the Медпу́нкт suggest?
3	What does the doctor do?
4	What's the treatment?

You will notice that there are two words for doctor. **Врач** is the usual word describing the profession, but you would usually use the word **до́ктор** when talking to one. You will see that the doctor says

'**Вы должны́ лежа́ть**' *You should lie down* and '**Вы должны́ отды-ха́ть**' *You should rest.* Here are some other examples of до́лжен-на-ны́ *ought, must*:

я до́лжен рабо́тать
ты до́лжен/должна́ отдыха́ть
она́ должна́ чита́ть
мы
вы должны́ лежа́ть
они́

Of course, the situation in a hotel is somewhat different from that experienced by non-tourists. An ordinary citizen would normally ring a *polyclinic* **поликли́ника** and would give his symptoms and his temperature over the telephone. The doctor might visit him or he might go to the polyclinic and see the doctor. He does not pay for treatment, but he will have to pay for the *medicines* **медикаме́нты** which he obtains from the *chemists* **апте́ка** on production of his *prescription* **реце́пт**.

There are many types of polyclinic in the Soviet Union — **де́тские** *children's*, **глазны́е** *eye*, **зубны́е** *dental*, гомеопати́ческие, физиотерапевти́ческие, гинекологи́ческие, и т.д. The three main kinds are:

1 Regional or municipal polyclinics
Райо́нные или городски́е поликли́ники

2 Polyclinics which belong to an organisation,
e.g. Поликли́ника Акаде́мии Нау́к СССР
Поликли́ника МГУ
Поликли́ника Комбина́та «Изве́стия» и т.д.

3 Пла́тные поликли́ники, in which you pay for treatment.

The usual polyclinics are similar in function to British health centres. The doctors who work in them are general practitioners, but some polyclinics have specialists. You will notice that it is possible to obtain treatment by paying for it at the polyclinic. This does not correspond to the 'private medicine' obtainable in the West, as the money goes to the State and not to the doctor providing the treatment. People go to these 'paying' polyclinics for special treatment or because they think they will get better or quicker treatment by paying for it.

Convalescence is often available at **санато́рии** *sanatoria, convalescent homes* and trips to these places are often arranged by trade unions at cut rates. There are also **дома́ о́тдыха** *rest homes*, which are often situated at *resorts* **куро́рты** on the Black Sea and elsewhere.

133

See Grammar notes (Cases) page 154

Как вы себя чувствуете? *How do you feel?* Feelings, of course, are not always matters of health. You can feel *hot* **жа́рко**, *cold* **хо́лодно**, *bored* **ску́чно**, *warm* **тепло́** or *good* **хорошо́**, or even *bad* **пло́хо**, etc. These are usually preceded by the 'dative' form **мне**, **вам**, etc.

2 In the exercise below the English is on the left. You have to find the corresponding Russian, place the appropriate number in the box in the second column and draw a line to the appropriate word in the third column, marking the same number in the box on the right.

1	I feel cold	☐	вам	пло́хо	☐
2	Do you (familiar) feel hot?	☐	нам	жа́рко	☐
3	He feels bored	☐	мне	ску́чно	☐
4	We feel bad	☐	тебе	хорошо́	☐
5	Do you feel good?	☐	ему	хо́лодно	☐

These expressions may be changed into questions simply by altering the intonation. You can also make them negative by adding **не** in the appropriate place.

Вам не хо́лодно?

Вам не жа́рко?

Ужа́сно *terrible* is one way of expressing disapproval, **отли́чно** *excellent*, approval. Another expression of disapproval is **как вам не сты́дно**! *You ought to be ashamed!*

3 Put the numbers in the appropriate boxes.

1	I'm hot	мне хо́лодно	☐
2	I'm ill	мне жа́рко	☐
3	I'm bored	мне сты́дно	☐
4	I'm ashamed	мне хорошо́	☐
5	I'm cold	мне ску́чно	☐
6	I feel warm	мне бо́льно	☐
7	I feel good	мне тепло́	☐

Western observers often feel that the feelings and behaviour of Russians are extreme. Extremes of sadness and depression, extremes of excitement and joy, extremes of tenderness and violence are all reflected in the works of Russian authors. Some put this down to the climate, others to the geography of the country and others to the Russian '*soul*' '**ру́сская душа́**'. The atmosphere of Chékhov, the introspection and suffering in Dostoévsky, the physical involvement in Tolstóy, the laughter through tears of Gógol', all these give the works of these writers a peculiarly 'Russian' flavour. The use of folk songs by composers, especially Glínka and Chaikóvsky, also tend to reflect reality. This reflection of reality has always been an aim of Russian writers, even before the Revolution.

'Escapism', surrealism and other such phenomena are not a feature of the Soviet artistic scene, although many of the romantic works (films, books, popular music, etc.) about the Revolution are reminiscent of the American interpretations of the wild west. The attachment to realism might be the reason why the most popular English authors in the Soviet Union are Dickens and Graham Greene. Of course, Russians do not neglect Shakespeare, whom they also regard as a great literary genius, and there are many excellent translations of Shakespeare in Russian. Pasternák, for example, produced many of these, and some of the greatest Russian actors have produced outstanding performances (e.g. Смоктуно́вский in Га́млет).

Summary

Well, we hope you do not fall ill in the Soviet Union, but if you do, you should not be completely out of your depth. Notice particularly how the dative of the personal pronouns, **мне**, **вам**, etc. is used with impersonal expressions.

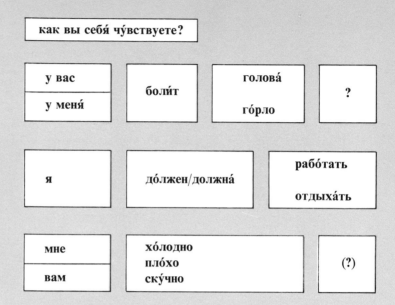

19

Reporting and registering

Read through the following passage. It is also on the recording.

Ле́то. О́чень жа́рко. Ми́ша и Ни́на смо́трят телеви́зор. В ко́мнате *stuffy* *boring* **ду́шно**, програ́мма **ску́чная**, и Ми́ша хо́чет пойти́ в бассе́йн. До бассе́йна далеко́, так как кварти́ра нахо́дится не в це́нтре го́рода. *lake* *bathe* Недалеко́ **о́зеро**. Там **купа́ться** не разреша́ется. Там всегда́ стои́т милиционе́р. Но так жа́рко, что невозмо́жно сиде́ть в ко́мнате. *fresh air* Они́ выхо́дят и гуля́ют у о́зера. Там, на **све́жем во́здухе**, хорошо́ и прия́тно.

О́коло о́зера

МИ́ША: Ни́на, хо́чешь искупа́ться?

to have a dip **НИ́НА:** О́чень хочу́, но здесь нельзя́ **купа́ться**. И у меня́ нет купа́льного костю́ма.

М: Ничего́... Всё ти́хо и споко́йно... Никого́ нет.

Н: Я не бу́ду.

М: А я бу́ду.

Н: Ми́ша, как тебе́ не сты́дно?!

trunks **М:** Почему́ мне должно́ быть сты́дно? На мне **пла́вки**. (вхо́дит в во́ду)
Ой, как хорошо́! Посмотри́, как я могу́ пла́вать! Класси́ческий стиль.

МИЛИЦИОНЕ́Р: Молодо́й челове́к! Сюда́, сюда́... Та-а-к...
Ва́ша фами́лия?

М: Ивано́в.

Мил: И́мя и о́тчество?

М: Михаи́л Бори́сович.

Мил: А́дрес?

М: Ерева́нская у́лица 6, кварти́ра 18.

Мил: Пройдёмте со мной.

М: Понима́ете, день тако́й жа́ркий...

talk **Мил:** Ничего́-ничего́... **Разгова́ривать** бу́дем не здесь.

М: Куда́ мы идём?

police station **Мил:** Куда́? В **мили́цию**, коне́чно.

137

В мили́ции.

КАПИТА́Н МИЛИ́ЦИИ: Так-так. Михаи́л Бори́сович Ивано́в.

birth Ерева́нская 6, кв 18. Год **рожде́ния?**

М: 1964. 16-го ма́рта.

Кап: Ме́сто рожде́ния?

М: Ки́ев.

Кап: Национа́льность?

М: Ру́сский.

Кап: (пи́шет всё э́то) Сего́дня у нас 16 ию́ля? Так, что там

happened **случи́лось?**

Мил: Граждани́н Ивано́в купа́лся в о́зере, а там купа́ться не разреша́ется.

Кап: Почему́ вы не пое́хали в бассе́йн?

lost money **М:** У меня́ де́нег нет… Я вчера́ **потеря́л де́ньги**… А сего́дня так жа́рко…

Кап: А вы не зна́ете, что там купа́ться нельзя́? Ведь вы ря́дом живёте!

М: Зна́ю, но…

dangerous **Кап:** Граждани́н Ивано́в, вы зна́ете, что в о́зере **опа́сно** пла́вать! Вы хорошо́ пла́ваете?

М: Не о́чень хорошо́, но все говоря́т, что у меня́ класси́ческий стиль…

must pay a fine **Кап:** Класси́ческий стиль! Вы **должны́ плати́ть штраф.**

М: Штраф!? Но у меня́ нет…

lose **Кап:** Где вы **потеря́ли** де́ньги? Когда́?

М: Вчера́ в кино́. Ка́жется, в буфе́те. Де́ньги бы́ли в чёрном

wallet **бума́жнике.** И па́спорт был там.

Кап: Граждани́н Ивано́в, ваш бума́жник нашли́. И мы вам звони́ли, но вас не бы́ло. Вот он. В бума́жнике ваш па́спорт и

sign пять рубле́й. **Распиши́тесь** здесь (пока́зывает) и плати́те штраф. Три рубля́.

М: Граждани́н капита́н, прости́те меня́. Я бо́льше не бу́ду.

next **Кап:** Ну, хорошо́, мо́жете идти́. Но по́мните, что в **сле́дующий** раз....

honestly **М: Че́стное сло́во**, я бо́льше не бу́ду. Спаси́бо вам. До свида́ния.

1 Now look at the following questionnaire (анке́та) and fill it in, according to the details that Misha gives to the sergeant in the recording.

АНКЕ́ТА

Фами́лия _____

И́мя и о́тчество _____

Да́та рожде́ния _____

Ме́сто рожде́ния _____

Национа́льность _____

А́дрес _____

Подпись _____

Да́та _____

---

2 Answer the following questions in English, based on the text and on the dialogue.

1	What was the television programme like?
2	Why did Misha want to go swimming?
3	Where did they decide to go?
4	Why didn't Nina want to bathe?
5	Why didn't Nina shout out?

6	Why couldn't they go to the swimming pool?
7	Where did Misha lose his money?
8	Where did it finally turn up?
9	How much was there?
10	What did the policeman finally tell Misha?

You will notice that some of the verbs in this unit have **-ся** or **-сь** on the end. These are called 'reflexive' verbs and correspond to the types of verb in English which have 'oneself', 'yourself', etc. after them, or understood. An example in the dialogue is **купа́ться** *to bathe* (lit. *bath oneself*).

If you go to the Soviet Union you will find that you have forms to fill in on various occasions. Travelling into the country you have to make a currency declaration which you should retain, as all currency transactions will be recorded on it and you will have to surrender it to the authorities when you leave. It is against the law to take rubles into or out of the Soviet Union, although it is possible to obtain travellers cheques in rubles abroad. There are shops in the Soviet Union which deal only in foreign currency as a direct way of attracting foreign currency into the Soviet Union. These are called **Берёзка** (lit. *birch tree*) shops, and many goods — drink, cigarettes, chocolates and fruit, are much cheaper if you buy them in *foreign currency* **валю́та**. But some things (records, books, fur hats, etc.) are more expensive because of their attractive packaging or higher than average quality. It may pay you to buy such items for rubles in a Russian store.

When you exchange money you will receive a form which you should keep in case you are asked for it on leaving the country. You should also keep receipts from the foreign currency shops. You may also need to fill in forms at the hotel where your passport will be retained for a day or two by the management. You will be issued with a **про́пуск** *pass*, which you will usually need to show to the porter to get back into the hotel.

Russians may be married in a *Registry Office* (**ЗАГС — За́пись**

áктов гражда́нского состоя́ния), a *Wedding Palace* (**Дворе́ц бракосочета́ний**) or in a church. Some couples, after they have set the date for their marriage in a Wedding Palace, receive a pass to enable them and their friends to buy goods in a special shop for newly-weds **магази́н для новобра́чных**. In Moscow the wedding party will often go to the tomb of the unknown soldier by the Kremlin wall to lay a wreath, or to the *Lenin Hills* **Ле́нинские Го́ры** by the University to have their photograph taken and drink champagne. At the registration stage the internal passport (which every Russian has) will be altered*.

Russians live in *flats* **кварти́ры** which divide into two categories: **госуда́рственные** *state* which may be **коммуна́льные** *communal* or self-contained, and **кооперати́вные** *co-operative* which are always self-contained. Rents for state flats vary according to the size of the flat. Co-operative flats are owned by the co-operative to which people pay a deposit and monthly repayments very much on the same lines as a mortgage repayment. More fortunate Russians may own their own **да́ча** or *country house*. Some of these are allocated by the state as a reward for services, but many of them are bought from savings. The old *communal flats* **коммуна́льные кварти́ры** where services are shared still exist in Moscow and other large cities, but they are not so common as they were twenty years ago. In order to live in a particular flat or to change flats, it is necessary to have a **пропи́ска** *a registration document or visa*. This is obtained at the *police station* **мили́ция**.

* Internal passports are compulsory from the age of 16. Many Russians carry them with them all the time. They are similar in function to the identity cards which British people carried during the war. International passports are obtained by special application.

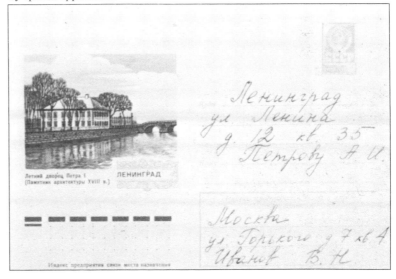

As you will see from the illustration overleaf, Russians have a different order for addressing letters than we do. First of all they put the country, then the town (sometimes with a district number), then the street, the number of the house, the flat number and finally the name of the person (in the dative) usually ending in **-y** for men and **-ой** for women. Then follow the initials.

3 ◧ Using the letter above as an example, address the envelope below to Миша, whom you met earlier in the unit.

Летний дворец Петра I ЛЕНИНГРАД
(Памятник архитектуры XVIII в.)

Куда

Кому

Индекс предприятия связи и адрес отправителя

Индекс предприятия связи места назначения

If you are addressing a letter to England, write it in the usual way but print **А́НГЛИЯ** opposite **Куда́** *where to....* There is also very often a space for the name of *the sender* **а́дрес отправи́теля**.

Summary

You should not now be taken by surprise at the number of forms you may have to fill in in the Soviet Union. You have also come across 'reflexive' verbs, which are fairly frequent in Russian. The ones that occur in this unit are mostly true reflexives, but occasionally you will find forms which are not, e.g. **случи́лось** *happened*.

20 | Revision

In the last four units we have been concentrating on topics which involve the expression of emotions, opinions and feelings, as well as looking at ways of reporting events. The following will help you assess your progress.

1 ◗ Here is a dialogue with some of the words missing. Put the appropriate numbers in the boxes beside the words supplied after the dialogue. The conversation is between a Leningrader and a Muscovite. They disagree about most things.

Ленинградец	Мне кажется, что в Ленинграде жить очень приятно. Улицы у нас широкие, здания красивые.
Москвич	В Москве тоже хорошо.
Ленинградец	Да, здесь хорошо, но в Ленинграде ____1____. Там прекрасные дворцы...
Москвич	В Москве тоже дворцы ____2____. Я ____3____ жить в Москве. Москва ____4____ СССР.
Ленинградец	Конечно, Москва чудесный город. Но Ленинград мне ____5____ нравится.
Москвич	Я тоже ____6____ что Ленинград чудесный город. Но в Москве ____7____ театров ____8____ кинотеатров, ____9____ ресторанов.
Ленинградец	Правда, у нас в Ленинграде ____10____ театров и ресторанов, но они не ____11____ , чем в Москве. Как тебе кажется?
Москвич	____12____ , ленинградец всегда предпочитает Ленинград, а москвич-Москву. Вот и всё!

столица	☐	хуже	☐	лучше	☐
думаю	☐	меньше	☐	прекрасные	☐
больше	☐ ☐ ☐	по-моему	☐	предпочитаю	☐

143

2a 📖 Greeting people. Look at the list of greetings on the left and connect them with the appropriate picture.

1   С Но́вым Го́дом!

2   С днём рожде́ния!

3   С пра́здником!

4   Прия́тного аппети́та!

5   Поздравля́ю!

b Fill in the greetings in the sentences below. You should be able to work them out from the context.

(i) В де́вять часо́в я пошёл в бюро́.

« _____ _____ » сказа́л дире́ктор.

« _____ , Ива́н Серге́евич, как вы _____ ?»

(ii) В рестора́не

Де́вушка — Вот ва́ши бифште́ксы.

Тури́ст — Спаси́бо.

Де́вушка — _____ _____

Тури́ст — _____

(iii) До свида́ния, и _____ до́брого.

_____ _____ -его.

(iv) Уже́ по́здно. Тебе́ ну́жно спать.

_____ _____

_____ _____

КРОССВÓРД

1		2		3	4	5		6	7	8		9		10	11	12
13			14			15				16		17				
	18				19		20		21							
		22		23		24	25				26			27		
28			29	30		31		32		33	34					
	35				36	37				38				39		
40	41				42		43		44				45		46	
47			48			49				50		51	52		53	
54		55		56			57	58					59			
	60	61	62		63	64	65		66		67					
	68					69		70				71				
72	73		74	75	76	77		78	79		80		81			
82		83	84	85					86			87				
88		89									90	91				
	92		93	94	95			96	97	98				99		
100		101														

146

Across

1 Где мóжно покупáть медикамéнты
5 Дóктор или _____
8 This is good for Russians
13 __ __ __ надцать = 12
14 What a Russian might call an
   English or American spinster
15 This goes with tea in Russia
17 This is one of the many in
   Leningrad
18 Flu
19 __ __ __ __ етский — Egyptian
21 Врач сказáл, что я дóлжен

   _____
22 We
23 Rice
25 Book by Dostoevsky
26 Alma-_____, a city in the
   USSR
28 Lights up buildings
30 Take care or you'll catch one of
   these
34 Founded the USSR
35 First name
36 To go on foot
38 It's time to go — Мне _____*
39 But
40 A stand for an exhibition
42 Well, cheerio, be seeing you —
   Ну, _____, до свидá-
   ния
44 Optician (ends in к)
45 He or it
47 Here
48 В Москвé есть маршрýтные

   _____
51 War and Peace is a magnum

   _____
54 О __ __ ен, is a Russian decoration
55 Дóктор вы́писал _____
58 Ни́на _____ дéньги в
   библиотéке
60 A Russian amp
64 Н __ __ __ онáльность. Рýсский
66 __ __ __ вет!
67 Soviet oil town
68 Some say he's a bit like a boy
   scout
69 __ __ имат = weather
70 A shop where photographic
   equipment is sold
71 Coastal resort on the Black Sea
72 Что _____ в Большóм
   Теáтре?
74 Как __ __. A drink
76 __ __ __ надцать. Unlucky for
   some!
79 Russian agreement
80 Short comrade
81 У меня бол__ __ головá
82 First two letters of Yaroslavl´
83 Ugandan general
86 This is what normally gets ful-
   filled, or over-fulfilled in factories
88 В __ооп__рке живýт ти́гры,
   крокоди́лы и т.д.
89 This is where a sick Russian
   would go
91 Zoë
92 Peace or world
93 A tartar leader
96 Ки__ __ теáтр
98 An American dance
100 On
101 Высóкая _____ is what
   you might have if you feel ill.

Down

1 This is where you register in a
   hotel
2 Takes temperatures
3 Cyprus
4 Таблéтки, usually
5 Everybody
6 Мóжно слýшать р__д__о.
7 Он хорóший спортсмéн, __е-
   __ __он мира
8 It's cold
9 Ugly mug! (Second letter о)
10 Имя Руставéли. (See Unit 14)
11 Russians pride themselves on
   г__ __теприи́мство
12 Как вам не _____!
16 No
17 Имя и óтчество _____?
18 Where
20 To go
24 __ветский
27 Place where you see pictures
29 Short for Татья́на. Та__ __
30 Pedagogical Institute __ __ __ин-
   ститýт
31 Скóлько _____ эта кни́-
   га?
32 «__ __ __ в Москвé хорóшие
   теáтры!» said the tourist to the
   Muscovite
33 Прия́тного _____. Eat
   well!
34 Спорт__ __ __ __ is a draw
37 __и__лом. Is what students get if
   they're good
41 To there
43 Останóв__ __ автóбуса
46 Мне óчень _____ эта
   прогрáмма
48 Скажи__ __ пожáлуйста, где
   здесь ресторáн?
49 Ballet by Хачатуря́н
50 Ленингрáд, конéчно, тóже кра-
   си́вый _____
52 Пéрвое мáя __ __ __здник в
   СССР
53 Что _____? What hap-
   pened?
56 Price
57 Where the policemen work
58 Здесь былá гру__ __а турúстов
59 Jacob
61 Ко__мун__ст
62 Он говори́т __ __-рýсски
63 __ __спýблика
65 Central Committee
71 Catfish sold live in Moscow*
73 A kind of play
75 They
77 Актёр исполня́ет _____
78 A Russian camera (starts with зе)
80 Админис__ __ __ __ор
83 __ __парáт. Camera.
84 Sea
85 К__ __о. Measurement
86 Мы уви́дели _____ (Nina)
87 Еврóпа и _____. The two
   continents of USSR
88 Ама__ __ __ка. Lady warrior
90 2
94 __ль__инист. Climber
95 Not
97 Кур__ __т. Resort
99 Паль__ __. Coat

147

3 ◼ Feeling well and feeling ill. Choose the alternative.

a   Иван бóлен. Он себя чýвствует
хорошó
сты́дно
плóхо

b   Нúна больнá. У
негó
вас   болúт гóрло.
неё

c   Закрóйте окнó. Мне здесь óчень
хóлодно
жáрко
теплó

d   Врач вы́писал мне рецéпт, и я пошёл в
медпýнкт
магазúн
аптéку

e   В аптéке мне дáли
вóду
медикамéнты
температýру

4 ◗ Here is a series of questions and answers about a person. Put the letter of the question in the box opposite the correct answer.

a	Фами́лия?	ул. Чайко́вского 5 кв. 18	☐
b	И́мя?	Ники́та Петро́вич	☐
c	О́тчество?	Москва́	☐
d	Да́та рожде́ния?	Су́слова	☐
e	Ме́сто рожде́ния?	Ники́тична	☐
f	А́дрес?	А́нна	☐
g	И́мя и о́тчество отца́?	А́нна Миха́йловна	☐
h	И́мя и о́тчество ма́тери?	Студе́нтка	☐
i	Национа́льность?	16ое апре́ля 1959 го́да	☐
j	Профе́ссия?	Ру́сская	☐

If you have managed to get this far and have been able to complete most of the tasks you have been set, you should know enough Russian to get around reasonably well in the Soviet Union. We hope above all that you have enjoyed learning a little Russian and a little about Russians as people.

До свида́ния.
Всего́ хоро́шего.

BBC production team and Soviet film crew on location in Moscow, filming for the television series 'Russian Language and People'

Using the course in classes

This book deliberately sets out to be different: it combines a serious attempt to teach a minimal amount of formal language with a great deal of information about the daily life and culture of the Russian people. It is not designed specifically for use with a teacher; indeed it is intended to be self-instructional, and therefore attempts to bypass the teacher altogether. This is not to say, however, that it might not be profitably used in formal teaching — in evening classes or schools.

Teachers may wish to exploit the television series broadcast when the book was first published, and may want to use the book to do this more effectively. They may wish to supplement their regular teaching, or even to start with the syllabus of the book, using the methodology explained in the Introduction, and perhaps add supplementary materials specific to their own purpose. Both book and programmes will, after all, be of interest to the type of student who is likely to enter an evening class, and the presence of a teacher should inevitably increase the effectiveness of the materials, especially if the following points are borne in mind:

1   The language content of the course is of limited scope, and we have deliberately tried to avoid grammatical technicalities. We have provided grammatical notes for the more academically inclined or curious student, but essentially the course relies on the initiative of the student to take him or her to the notes, rather than suggesting that these are the rules that are necessary in order to learn Russian. The syllabus exploits some of the common factors between English and Russian, to help convince the student that he can extract information from Russian texts (spoken or written), which might be of use to him in the Soviet Union. We believe that new supplementary exercises based on the acquisition of information will be more useful than those intended to refine pronunciation or deepen knowledge of grammar. The adult learner has already acquired a variety of skills in his own language, particularly in extracting the gist meaning from written or spoken language. The problem is how to transfer this to the learning of a foreign language. The use of authentic source materials in this course is designed to reinforce such skills. **Comprehension** is the focal point of the course, and it is assumed in this context that vocabulary is more important than grammar in understanding language, especially in the printed form. The crossword puzzles have been devised with this specifically in mind.

2   The principles on which the syllabus has been constructed are those of the 'communicative approach' — i.e. they concentrate not on teaching 'correct' language according to grammatical rules but on

helping the learner to be able to say and understand what he needs to in a selected number of foreseeable situations.

This means that **functions** (greetings, congratulations, getting about, giving opinions, etc.) are the starting point, and that grammatical features play a secondary role. Such features as perfectives do occur in the course, but it is not necessary to understand the whole system of aspects in order to decipher their meaning. We have tried to grade the grammatical content as far as possible but we have always based the material on the spoken and written language as it occurs in contemporary contexts.

3   Many of the activities which the learner is asked to carry out are based on the extraction of information from texts that he may not fully understand. He is given enough linguistic information to enable him to extract the parts of a text that might be of use to him, and he is helped by the fact that the texts have been selected so as to contain easily guessable words. The title and format of the text are also short cuts towards the retrieval of information. Texts giving information about entertainments, radio, television and sport, for example, are all rich in related words or cognates, and teachers should bear these subjects in mind when selecting supplementary material. Scientific texts, too, have similar characteristics and lend themselves to a comprehension-based approach.

We believe that the learner who has worked conscientiously through this book, with or without a teacher, will have a first basis for consolidating his knowledge of the Russian language, and developing a variety of language skills: for example the accompanying sound recordings may be used not only to develop comprehension of the spoken word but also to encourage the learner to make his or her first steps in speaking. Above all, of course, the student should **enjoy** his first attempts at learning Russian, and we hope that teachers will also enjoy introducing students to the language via *Russian — language and people.*

Alphabet: *transliteration and pronunciation guide.*

Russian

Large	Small	Transliteration	Approximate pronunciation (where different or unexpected)
А	а	a	
Б	б	b	
В	в	v	
Г	г	g	*'v' when between two vowels as in его, -ого.*
Д	д	d	
Е	е	ye**	*ye as in yet*
Ё	ё	yo***	
Ж	ж	zh	*like 's' in pleasure*
З	з	z	
И	и	i	*like 'ee' in sweet*
Й	й	i or y	*like y in boy*
К	к	k	
Л	л	l	
М	м	m	
Н	н	n	
О	о	o	
П	п	p	
Р	р	r	*rolled (Scottish)*
С	с	s	
Т	т	t	
У	у	u	*'oo' in boot*
Ф	ф	f	
Х	х	kh	*'h' but hard like Scottish 'loch'*
Ц	ц	ts	
Ч	ч	ch	*but very occasionally 'sh' as in что (shto)*
Ш	ш	sh	
Щ	щ	shch	
Ъ	ъ	hard sign*	
Ы	ы	y	*like y in 'physio-'*
Ь	ь	soft sign*	
Э	э	e	*E in Edward*
Ю	ю	yu	
Я	я	ya	

* May be written ′ or omitted.
** Initially and after vowels except y, otherwise e.
*** In all positions except after ch and shch, when o is used.

This is not, strictly speaking, a guide for pronunciation, although it may be used as an approximate guide. If it be so used, care should be taken not to change the sounds in an English way. For example, some English speakers might be tempted to pronounce the Russian word 'kosmos' as if it had 'z' where the first 's' is. A nearer approximation to the sound of the word in Russian might be represented in English by 'kossmoss'. There are many other examples of this. What is most important in Russian is that you should STRESS words in the right place. Stress in Russian is much stronger than in English, and changes the sound in a much more basic way. The sound under the stress is always given its full value, but vowels in other positions often sound very different from what you would expect, e.g. the 'o' sounds in 'хорошо' (khoroshó). Listen carefully to the recordings.

Approximate Pronunciation Guide for Alphabet Units 1–5

Unit 1

1	KOMÉTA	12	PIANÍST
2	TASS	13	VINÓ
3	SSSR (Es Es Es Air)	14	MOSKVÁ
4	KÁSSA	15	RESTORÁN
5	TEÁTR	16	ORKÉSTR
6	ÁTOM	17	ÁVIA
7	METRÓ	18	MÁRKA
8	ÓPERA	19	APPARÁT
9	SPORT	20	NET
10	PARK	21	STOP
11	TAKSÍ		

Unit 2

1	VODÁ	8	KOMMUNÍZM	15	DÁTA
2	VÓDKA	9	LÉNIN	16	KVAS
3	LIMONÁD	10	PRÁVDA	17	APTÉKA
4	LITR	11	KROKODÍL	18	MIR
5	KILÓ	12	KAVKÁZ	19	KIÓSK
6	KILOMÉTR	13	ZO-OPÁRK*	20	TOLSTÓY
7	UNIVERSITÉT	14	DOM	21	SOVÉTSKY

* Two o's pronounced separately.

Unit 3

1	FUTBÓL	11	TELEFÓN	22	UZBÉK
2	KLUB	12	BULYÓN	23	KLÍMAT
3	SOYÚZ	13	SOVÉTSKY SOYÚZ	24	DINÁMO
4	PROFSOYÚZ	14	KAFÉ	25	STADIÓN
5	FÁBRIKA	15	BYURÓ	26	SPARTÁK
6	VKHOD (fhod)	16	FÓTO	27	TORPÉDO*
7	KOSTYÚM	17	KREML'	28	LOKOMOTÍV
8	VDNH	18	FIL'M	29	REMÓNT
	(Vay Day En Ha)	19	YÚMOR	30	ADMINISTRÁTOR
9	MENYÚ	20	AVTÓBUS	31	HOKKÁY
10	PEREHÓD	21	BUFÉT	32	KINÓ

* Not like English, more like TORPYÉDO.

Unit 4

1	GÓROD	11	GUM	20	ÓL'GA
2	TELEGRÁMMA	12	EKSPRÉSS	21	MAY (like Eng. My)
3	GOD	13	ENÉRGIYA	22	NEDÉLYA
4	TURÍSTY	14	PROGRÁMMA	23	RYAD
5	AEROFLÓT*	15	PÉRVAYA	24	BLANK
6	SAMOLYÓT		PROGRÁMMA	25	INTURÍST
7	EKSKÚRSIYA	16	VÝHOD	26	MGU (Em Gay OO)
8	IZVÉSTIYA	17	VYHODÍT'	27	MÉSTO (MYÉSTO)
9	GAZÉTA	18	GRIBÝ		
10	ROSSÍYA	19	ÓRDEN		

* A and E pronounced separately.

Unit 5

1	CHÉHOV	12	BOL'SHOY TEÁTR	22	KHRUSHCHÓV
2	CHÁIKA	13	MOSKVÍCH	23	SHCHI
3	MASHÍNA	14	ETÁZH	24	SHÁPKA
4	ELEKTRÍCHESTVO	15	MÓZHNO	25	ZHÉNSHCHINA
5	ELEKTRIFIKÁTSIYA	16	HOROSHÓ	26	TSYRK
6	INFORMÁTSIYA	17	SHOSSÉ	27	PÓCHTA
7	BIFSHTÉKS	18	TSVETÝ	28	TSK (TseyKA)
8	SHASHLÝK	19	KURYÁSHCHIY	29	TSENTR
9	DEMONSTRÁTSIYA	20	NEKURYÁSHCHIY	30	KONTSÉRT
10	MATCH	21	KRÁSNAYA	31	BUL'VÁR
11	DVORETS S'YÉZDOV		PLÓSHCHAD'		

Grammar Notes

1 Genders Russian has three genders — masculine, feminine and neuter. Usually the gender can be recognised from the ending (see *page 156*).

2 Cases Russian nouns, adjectives and pronouns have six cases. This means that words change their endings according to their function in a sentence. The cases are as follows:

1 *Nominative* The 'naming' case. This is the one you will find in the dictionary. It is used for the subject of a sentence.

2 *Accusative* Used for the direct object of a sentence and after some prepositions, notably в (into) and на (onto) and чéрез (across). Also used in many time expressions, either on its own or with a preposition. Is identical in form with the genitive in masculine 'animate' nouns (i.e. referring to people) but in 'inanimate' (i.e. referring to objects) masculine nouns and neuter nouns it is identical in form with the nominative.

154

3 *Genitive* The 'possession' case, or the 'of' case. It is used with a large number of prepositions (из, от, с, у, etc.) and after numerals (see *page 162*). It can sometimes also occur as the direct object of a negative verb.

4 *Dative* The 'giving' case (e.g. Он дал мне книгу — *he gave* **me** *a book*), or the 'for' case (e.g. **Он купил мне книгу** — *he bought* **me** *a book*), or the 'to' case (e.g. **Он мне звонил** — *he rang* (to) *me*). Used after many prepositions, notably **к** *to, towards* and **по** *along*.

5 *Instrumental* The 'with' or 'by' case. Used on its own to indicate the instrument used (e.g. **Он писал карандашóм** — *he was writing with a pencil*) and after some prepositions, notably **с** *with* (**чай с молокóм** — *tea with milk*, **салат с грибáми** — *salad with mushrooms*). Also used on its own in certain time expressions (**вéчером, веснóй**, etc.).

6 *Prepositional* or *Locative*. The 'place' case. Only used after prepositions, the main ones of which are **в** *in*, **на** *on*, **о** *about* and **при** (belonging to *or* in the time of).

3 **Prepositions** All cases, except the Nominative, may have prepositions before them, i.e. they may be 'governed' by a preposition. Here is a list of some of the main prepositions with their cases.

Accusative	**в** *into*, **на** *onto*, **за** *in exchange for*
Genitive	**у** *by/at*, **из** *out of*, **от** *from*, **до** *as far as/up to*, **с** *from*, **для** *for*, **без** *without*
Dative	**к** *towards*, **по** *along, about* etc.
Instrumental	**с** *with*, **под** *under*, **над** *above*, **за** *for*
Locative	**в** *in*, **на** *on*, **о** *about*

4 **Endings:** Nouns. You can very often tell which gender a noun belongs to by looking at the ending of the nominative case. Here is a list of all the endings of this case grouped by gender.

Masculine	Feminine	Neuter
consonant	-а	-о
-й	-я	-е
-ь	-ь	-ие
	-ия	-мя

These appear in nouns which are of Russian origin or in nouns of foreign origin which have become 'russified' (**футбóл, чай, машúна**, etc.). Words which have not (yet) changed in form often do not change their endings at all (**таксú, кенгурý, кинó**, etc.).

5 **Tables** Notice that many of the forms below are parallel, in that they involve a change in one letter only and this is usually a corresponding vowel. To help you, here is a list of the ten Russian vowels, divided into two sets. The arrows represent the usual changes that take place.

English	Russian	
a	а ——————→ я	
e	э	↗ е ↘
i	ы ————→ и	
o	о ————————→ ё ↙	
u	у ——————→ ю	

Notice that ё is always stressed.

6 **Nouns:** Masculine

	Singular	*Plural*
Nom.	теа́тр	теа́тры
Acc.	теа́тр*	теа́тры*
Gen.	теа́тра	теа́тров
Dat.	теа́тру	теа́трам
Instr.	теа́тром	теа́трами
Loc.	(в) теа́тре	(в) теа́трах

	Singular	*Plural*
Nom.	геро́й	геро́и
Acc.	геро́я*	геро́ев*
Gen.	геро́я	геро́ев
Dat.	геро́ю	геро́ям
Instr.	геро́ем	геро́ями
Loc.	(о) геро́е	(о) геро́ях

* In inanimate nouns the accusative is like the nominative. In animate nouns it is like the genitive.

Note. Masculine nouns in -ь *behave like* **геро́й**, *except that they end in* -ей *in the genitive plural.*

7 **Nouns:** Feminine

	Singular	*Plural*
Nom.	фа́брика	фа́брики
Acc.	фа́брику	фа́брики
Gen.	фа́брики	фа́брик*
Dat.	фа́брике	фа́брикам
Instr.	фа́брикой	фа́бриками
Loc.	(на) фа́брике	(на) фа́бриках

	Singular	Plural
Nom.	пло́щадь	пло́щади
Acc.	пло́щадь	пло́щади
Gen.	пло́щади	площаде́й*
Dat.	пло́щади	площадя́м
Instr.	пло́щадью	площадя́ми
Loc.	(на) пло́щади	(на) площадя́х

Feminine nouns ending in **-я** behave very much like the ones in **-а**, but they have *soft* endings e.g. **Та́ня → Та́ню** (*Acc.*) → **с Та́ней** (*Instr.*). The ones in **-ия** have **-ий** in the genitive plural, and **-ии** in the Locative singular.

8   Nouns: Neuter

Notice that many of the neuter nouns we have used do not change their endings (**кино́, метро́, Дина́мо, кило́, фо́то, кафе́, бюро́, Торпе́до**). One that does change is **ме́сто** *place*.

	Singular	Plural
Nom.	ме́сто	места́
Acc.	ме́сто	места́
Gen.	ме́ста	мест
Dat.	ме́сту	места́м
Instr.	ме́стом	места́ми
Loc.	(на) ме́сте	(на) места́х

The singular of neuter nouns is very much like the masculine singular. Neuter nouns are always inanimate. The genitive plural is very much like feminine in -a (it has a 'zero' ending).

	Singular	Plural
Nom.	свида́ние	свида́ния
Acc.	свида́ние	свида́ния
Gen.	свида́ния	свида́ний
Dat.	свида́нию	свида́ниям
Instr.	свида́нием	свида́ниями
Loc.	свида́нии	свида́ниях

If you want to learn these off by heart, it would help if you notice that in all instances the Dative, Instrumental and Locative plurals are very similar in form. The same is true with adjectives. Not all types of noun are listed above. If you want a more comprehensive list, you should consult any standard grammar of Russian.

9 Adjectives

These are much simpler than nouns, in that there are not as many classes, and the plural tends to be the same for all three genders. Masculine and neuter are very much alike, so we have put them together.

	Masculine	Neuter	Feminine	Plural
Nom.	интере́сный	интере́сное	интере́сная	интере́сные
Acc.	интере́сный*	интере́сное*	интере́сную	интере́сные*
Gen.	интере́сного		интере́сной	интере́сных
Dat.	интере́сному		интере́сной	интере́сным
Instr.	интере́сным		интере́сной	интере́сными
Loc.	интере́сном		интере́сной	интере́сных

* Same rule as for nouns (page 156).

Notice that in the feminine all the last four endings are the same, and notice also the similarity between adjectival and noun endings, with '**-ы**' taking the place of '**a**' in the Dative, Instrumental and Locative plural.

In some adjectives, e.g. **вече́рний**, the endings are all soft, so you have a straight substitution of '**я**' for '**a**', '**e**' for '**o**', etc. — **вече́рняя газе́та** and **я чита́л вече́рнюю газе́ту**, etc. Another feature you might notice is in such expressions as **в на́шем но́мере**, **в хоро́шем го́роде**. This occurs because Russians do not normally write an unstressed '**o**' after **ж, ч, ш, щ** and **ц**.
Look at the following.

	Masculine	Neuter	Feminine	Plural
Nom.	хоро́ший	хоро́шее	хоро́шая	хоро́шие
Acc.	хоро́ший*	хоро́шее	хоро́шую	хоро́шие*
Gen.	хоро́шего		хоро́шей	хоро́ших
Dat.	хоро́шему		хоро́шей	хоро́шим
Instr.	хоро́шим		хоро́шей	хоро́шими
Loc.	хоро́шем		хоро́шей	хоро́ших

NB. Note that some adjectives have a short form and this is much simpler than the long form, but it is only used in the 'predicate' of a sentence, e.g.

ресторáн откры́т	*The restaurant is open*
кафé закры́то	*The cafe is closed*
они́ откры́ты	*They are open*

10 Adverbs are usually derived from adjectives, by taking off the ending and adding **-о**

хоро́ший → хорошо́ *well*
плохо́й → пло́хо *badly*
интере́сный → интере́сно *interesting*

11 Comparison

We have used a few short forms of the comparative, as follows:–

хорошо́ → лу́чше *better*
пло́хо → ху́же *worse*
большо́й → бо́льше *bigger, more*
and ме́ньше *less*

followed by a simple genitive or **чем** *than.*

12 Pronouns

Singular

Nom.		я	ты	(он) оно	она
Acc.		меня	тебя	его	её
Gen.		меня	тебя	его	её
Dat.		мне	тебе	ему	ей
Instr.		мной	тобой	им	ей/ею
Loc.	(обо) мне		(о) тебе	(о) нём	(о) ней

Plural

Nom.		мы	вы	они
Acc.		нас	вас	их
Gen.		нас	вас	их
Dat.		нам	вам	им
Instr.		нами	вами	ими
Loc.	(о) них		(о) вас	(о) них

Notice that when the pronoun begins with a vowel and is governed by a preposition, **н** is added, e.g. **о нём, у них** (gen.), etc.

13 Possessive Pronouns

These behave like adjectives and have the same endings as хороший, except in the following cases.

				pl.
Nom.	ваш	ваша	ваше	ваши
Acc.	ваш	вашу	ваше	ваши
(like ваш is наш)				
Nom.	мой	моя	моё	мои
Acc.	мой	мою	моё	мои

14 Verbs: Infinitives

The part of the verb you will normally meet in a dictionary is the one which usually ends in -ть. — рабо́тать, гуля́ть, говори́ть, смотре́ть, etc. It is often possible to tell from the infinitive how the endings are going to change. Look at the examples below.

Present Tense

чита́ть		говори́ть	
я	чита́ю	я	говорю́
ты	чита́ешь	ты	говори́шь
он	чита́ет	он	говори́т
мы	чита́ем	мы	говори́м
вы	чита́ете	вы	говори́те
они	чита́ют	они	говоря́т
stem чита́-		*stem* говор-	

In some verbs the stem is slightly different from the infinitive form. If you know the first and second persons singular, you can usually guess the rest. Look at the examples below.

е́хать		идти́	
я	е́ду	я	иду́
ты	е́дешь	ты	идёшь
он	е́дет	он	идёт
мы	е́дем	мы	идём
вы	е́дете	вы	идёте
они	е́дут	они	иду́т

There are one or two exceptions to the above, notably the following:

хоте́ть	
я	хочу́
ты	хо́чешь
он	хо́чет
мы	хоти́м
вы	хоти́те
они	хотя́т

Past tenses are usually formed from the infinitive, by taking away
-ть and adding -л, -ла, -ло, -ли depending on the gender and number
of the person involved.

я (masc.) он Ивáн	читáл говорúл
я (fem.) онá Вéра	читáла говорúла
мы вы онú	читáли говорúли

онó   After онó, or neuter nouns, the past tense ends in -ло,
e.g. оно было, радио Москва говорило.

(Exception: идти → шёл   шла   шли)

15   Verbs: Imperatives

Imperatives are formed by taking the stem of the present tense: if it
ends in a vowel, add **-й** or **-йте**. If it ends in a consonant, add **-и** or
-ите.

Thus,

читáй (the 'ты' form) читáйте   *read!*
говорú   говорúте   *speak!*
идú   идúте   *go!*

Пойдём (let's go!) is also an imperative.

16   Verbs: Aspects

Most Russian verbs have two aspects, the Imperfective and the
Perfective. Forms of both of these occur in the course. The Imperfective is used for the present tense and the compound future.* The
Perfective is used for the simple future and in the past to show that
an action is complete, or that it is modified in some way. Some
examples of pairs are as follows:

IMPERF. покупáть   смотрéть   éхать
PERF.   купúть   посмотрéть   поéхать

Aspects are not a major feature of this course and should not be
treated as such. A realisation that the term exists is enough at the
present stage.

*
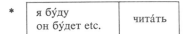

| я бýду
он бýдет etc. | читáть |

161

17 Numerals

1	оди́н одна́ (fem.) одно́ (neut.)
2	два две (fem.)
3	три
4	четы́ре
5	пять
6	шесть
7	семь
8	во́семь
9	де́вять
10	де́сять
11	оди́ннадцать
12	двена́дцать
13	трина́дцать
14	четы́рнадцать
15	пятна́дцать
16	шестна́дцать
17	семна́дцать
18	восемна́дцать
19	девятна́дцать
20	два́дцать
21	два́дцать оди́н
22	два́дцать два
23	два́дцать три *etc.*
30	три́дцать
40	со́рок
50	пятьдеся́т
60	шестьдеся́т
70	се́мьдесят
80	во́семьдесят
90	девяно́сто
100	сто
200	две́сти
300	три́ста
400	четы́реста
500	пятьсо́т
600	шестьсо́т
700	семьсо́т
800	восемьсо́т
900	девятьсо́т
1000	ты́сяча
1,000,000	миллио́н

After оди́н/одна́/одно́ the nom. sg. is used; after два/две, три, четы́ре (and numerals ending in these) the gen. sg. is used; after numerals other than these, the gen. pl. is used (see p. 60).

18 Word building

It is often possible to guess the meaning of a word by breaking it down into its component parts, i.e. prefix, root and ending. Roots can only be learned by constant exposure to Russian. Here are some useful prefixes with approximate meanings:

без- бес-	*without*	беспла́тно *free, i.e. without paying*
в-	*into (en-)*	вход *entrance*
вз- вс- вос-	*upwards*	взлёт *take-off*
вы-	*out of (ex-)*	вы́ход *exit*
до-	*up to*	дочита́ть *to read to the end*
за-	*for (purpose)*	заходи́те! *come and see us!*
	in exchange for	зарпла́та *wages*
из- ис-	*from*	и́здали *from a long way away*
между-	*inter-*	междунаро́дный *international*
на-	*onto*	напра́во *to the right*
не- ни-	*not un-*	негра́мотность *illiteracy*
о- об-	*about*	описа́ть *describe*
от	*from*	отходи́ть *to go away*
пере-	*across trans- re-*	перехо́д *crossing*
по-	*a little*	почита́ть *read a little*
при-	*towards*	прие́зд *arrival*
про-	*through for*	продава́ть *sell*
раз- рас-	*separation*	ра́зный *different*
с- со-	*with together from*	съезд *meeting* сходи́ть *to alight*
у-	*away from*	уходи́ть *to go away*

Suffixes are added after the stem and can tell you something about the word itself. **-ция** can often be translated as *-tion* as can **-ность**. Other common ones are **-тель** (*often -er*) чита́тель (*reader*). Another common one is **-ник** (спу́тник), the feminine form of which is **-ница**, and **-ец**. Other suffixes, of course, are the endings listed in the rest of the grammar section. These give you information about whether the word is a verb, a noun, etc. and of its number, gender, case or person.

Key to exercises

Unit 1

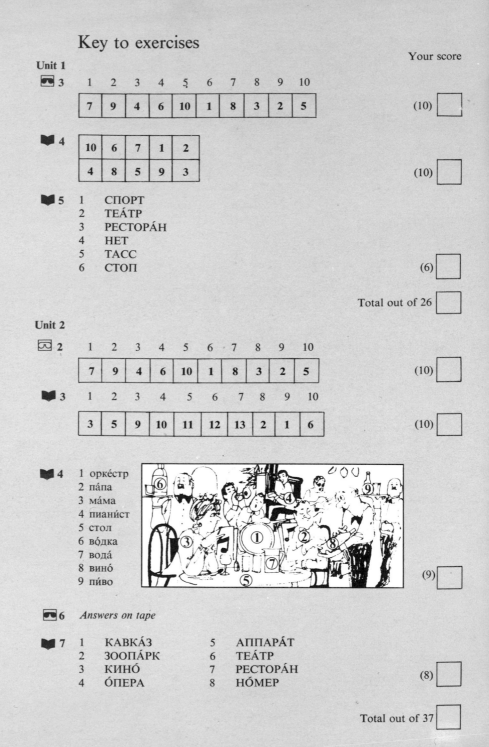

3

1	2	3	4	5	6	7	8	9	10
7	9	4	6	10	1	8	3	2	5

(10)

4

10	6	7	1	2
4	8	5	9	3

(10)

5
1 СПОРТ
2 ТЕА́ТР
3 РЕСТОРА́Н
4 НЕТ
5 ТАСС
6 СТОП

(6)

Total out of 26

Unit 2

2

1	2	3	4	5	6	7	8	9	10
7	9	4	6	10	1	8	3	2	5

(10)

3

1	2	3	4	5	6	7	8	9	10
3	5	9	10	11	12	13	2	1	6

(10)

4
1 орке́стр
2 па́па
3 ма́ма
4 пиани́ст
5 стол
6 во́дка
7 вода́
8 вино́
9 пи́во

(9)

6 *Answers on tape*

7
1 КАВКА́З
2 ЗООПА́РК
3 КИНО́
4 О́ПЕРА
5 АППАРА́Т
6 ТЕА́ТР
7 РЕСТОРА́Н
8 НО́МЕР

(8)

Total out of 37

Unit 3

⬛ 1 1 | 16 | 2 | 7 | 3 | 9 | 4 | 14 | 5 | 20 |

6 | 32 | 7 | 25 | 8 | 21 | 9 | 11 | 10 | 2 | (10) ☐

📖 1 | 20 | 2 | 10 | 3 | 25 | 4 | 12 | 5 | 11 |

6 | 31 | 7 | 22 | 8 | 15 | 9 | 19 | 10 | 27 | (10) ☐

📖 2 | ← | → | ← | → |

| → | ← | ← | → | (8) ☐

⬛ 3 1 | → | ← | ↑ |

2 | ↑ | → | ← | ↑ | √ |

3 | → | → | ↑ |

4 | ← | → | → | √ |

5 | → | → | ← | ↑ | (5) ☐

📖 4 1 | 4 |

2 | 5 |

3 | 5 |

4 | 3 |

5 | 1 | (5) ☐

📖 5 2 ↑ 7 ← 1 → 4
3 ← 3 → 6 ← 1
4 ↑ 7 → 1 ← 8 → 6
5 → 5 ← 2 (4) ☐

⬛ 6 1 No
2 tomorrow
3 always
4 for repairs
5 Beer, wine and vodka (5) ☐

165

📖 7 1 ФУТБÓЛ
    2 КАФÉ
    3 ФÓТО
    4 БЮРÓ
    5 СОЮ́З   (5) ☐

📖 8 1 МЕНЮ́
    2 ДИНÁМО
    3 ПЕРЕХÓД
    4 ФÁБРИКА
    5 УНИВЕРСИТÉТ   (5) ☐

Total out of 57 ☐

Unit 4

1	2	3	4	5	6	7	8	9	10
16	11	20	6	2	18	24	19	4	9

1	2	3	4	5	6	7	8	9	10
18	8	16	23	17	10	2	6	13	5

(20) ☐

📖 1 No smoking! No entry. No photography. No exit.
No smoking here! No crossing. Don't walk on the grass! (7) ☐

👓 2 1 Natasha   4 To go to the theatre
    2 Yes   5 Not today, she's busy
    3 Igor   6 Tomorrow   (6) ☐

📖 3 1 ГРИБЫ́
    2 ПРОГРÁММА
    3 ЭНÉРГИЯ
    4 АЭРОФЛÓТ
    5 ÓРДЕН   6 | Г | Ó | Р | О | Д | (6) ☐

📖 4 1 ГАЗÉТА
    2 ИНТУРИ́СТ
    3 ЭКСПРÉСС
    4 РОССИ́Я
    5 ЭКСКУ́РСИЯ
    6 ИЗВÉСТИЯ   7 | Т | У | Р | Й | С | Т | (7) ☐

📖 5 1 САМОЛЁТ
    2 БИЛÉТ
    3 ПÉРВАЯ
    4 ВЫ́ХОД
    5 НЕДÉЛЯ   (5) ☐

    Total out of 51 ☐

	1	2	3	4	5	6	7	8	9	10
	4	14	25	21	19	12	30	7	31	18

(10) ☐

	1	2	3	4	5	6	7	8	9	10
	18	7	17	24	14	23	25	19	29	8

(10) ☐

1 Во Дворце́ Съе́здов идёт бале́т
Во па́рке идёт конце́рт
В университе́те идёт ле́кция
В кино́ идёт фильм
В Большо́м теа́тре идёт о́пера   (5) ☐

2 1 МО́ЖНО
2 ПО́ЧТА
3 ЧЕ́ХОВ
4 ХРУЩЁВ
5 МУЖЧИ́НА   6 | О́ | П | Е | Р | А | (6) ☐

3 1 ЧА́ЙКА
2 ШОССЕ́
3 ИНФОРМА́ЦИЯ
4 ЦЕНТР
5 ЖЕ́НЩИНА
6 ХОРОШО́
7 МАТЧ   8 | К | О | Н | Ц | Е́ | Р | Т | (8) ☐

Total out of 39 ☐

Revision

a Он в теа́тре
Она́ в па́рке
Они́ в па́рке
Оно́ в Ленингра́де
Она́ в Москве́
Он в зоопа́рке
Она́ в апте́ке
Он в рестора́не
Он в кварти́ре
Он в автома́те   (10) ☐

b в це́нтре Москвы́
входи́ть
входи́ть
вхо́да
матч   (5) ☐

c

D	F
H	J
A	E
I	B
C	G

(10) ☐

Total out of 25 ☐

Unit 6

👓 **1**

Vodka	*tea*	*postcard*
4р. 10 к.	1р. 5 к.	8к.

ticket	*stamps*	*camera*
4р. 00 к.	2р. 7 к.	10р. 8 к.

(6) ☐

👓 **2**
1. Tickets for the Bolshoi
2. The Bolshoi is closed
3. Palace of Congresses
4. There is a ballet showing
5. Three
6. Nine roubles

(6) ☐

Crossword

Across 1 ДЕВЯТЬ 4 ЦК 6 НЕТ 7 Я 9 ТРИ 11 ДА 12 БАЛЕТ
14 В 15 ШАПКА 18 ЭТАЖ 20 АВТОМАТ 22 ЩИ 23 ОН
24 НОМЕР 26 БУФЕТ 28 ГУМ 29 ТАСС 31 ОДЕССА 32 СТОП
33 МОТОР 34 ОНА
Down 1 ДЕВУШКА 2 ВОТ 3 ТРИ 5 КАФЕ 8 ОНО 10 РОК
13 МИР 14 ВЫ 16 ПЛАНЕТА 17 АВТОБУС 18 ЭТОТ
19 ДИНАМО 21 АНЕКДОТ 25 РИГА 27 СССР 29 ТОТ 30 СУП

Exercises in crossword

a

ШÁПКА НА ДÉВУШКЕ
БАЛÉТ В РИ́ГЕ
МОТÓР В АВТÓБУСЕ

b

ТРИ	НОМЕР ДЕВЯТЬ
Я	НОМЕР СЕМЬ
ДЕВУШКА	НОМЕР ОДИН
ВОТ	НОМЕР ДВА
КАФЕ	НОМЕР ПЯТЬ
НЕТ	НОМЕР ШЕСТЬ
ТРИ	НОМЕР ТРИ
	НОМЕР ВОСЕМЬ
	НОМЕР ДЕСЯТЬ

(12) ☐

Total out of 24 ☐

Unit 7

📖 1

4
2
5
1
3

(5) ☐

2 1 Vera
2 Postcards
3 Five
4 Engineer
5 Ten

(5) ☐

📖 3 1 Óльга Кóрбут совéтская спортсмéнка.
2 Ни́кон япóнский фотоаппара́т.
3 Дéвушка, у вас есть кра́сное винó?
4 Джон-Пóль II пéрвый пóльский Па́па.
5 На столé совéтское шампа́нское.
6 Дина́мовцы хорóшие футболи́сты.
7 Нью-Йóрк Таймс америка́нская газéта.
8 Бори́с совéтский дóктор.*
9 Одéсса украи́нский порт.
10 Ма́нчестер англи́йский гóрод.
(Other combinations are possible, but make sure they all fit in!)

(10) ☐

📖 4 1 Russian   5 Georgian
2 English   6 African
3 Chinese   7 Japanese
4 American   8 Uzbek

(8) ☐

■ 5 СУВЕНИРЫ   ФОТОГРАФИЯ

(2) ☐

Total out of 30 ☐

Unit 8

📖 1 Я игра́ю в футбóл
Он говори́т по-англи́йски
Вы гуля́ете в па́рке
Они говоря́т по-ру́сски
Он лю́бит игра́ть на гита́ре
Я смотрю́ телеви́зор
Мне нра́вится танцева́ть

(7) ☐

2 1 Doctor
2 Walking in the park
3 Watches television
4 Sport and films
5 Ice hockey
6 He doesn't like it (6) ☐

3 1 18.20   6 15.25
2 21.05   7 17.03
3 22.10   8 13.16
4 19.15   9 14.29
5 12.22 10 10.20 (10) ☐

4 1 14.00 часо́в/два часа́
2 13.00 часо́в/час
3 20.00 часо́в/во́семь часо́в
4 07.00 часо́в
5 06.00 часо́в (5) ☐

5 2 21.00 'Time' — Information programme
3 19.10 'Moscow and the Muscovites'
4 18.25 Concert — Ukrainian Choir
5 22.20 Draw for Sport lotto
6 21.30 Evening of poetry by Yu. Drunina
7 18.15 Waltzes of Chaikovsky played by the orchestra
          of the Bolshoi Theatre (6) ☐

6 1 Filmed concert. Oistrakh plays Mozart.
2 19.15
3 'Time' Information programme
4 Poetry of Yevtushenko (4) ☐

7   ШЕКСПИР
       ОКТЯБРЬ
       УАСЫ (3) ☐

Total out of 41 ☐

Unit 9
1 A 7.40   B 7.93
   C 3.10   D 7.82 (4) ☐

2 1 Pekin
2 There's a big delegation from Japan there
3 Ukrainian hotel
4 Twenty minutes
5 Fillet Cosmos, 'Ministry' cutlets, white wine (5) ☐

3

8	7	9	6	3

10	5	4	2	1

(10) ☐

170

4 a 7.40 b 7.93
c 3.10 d 7.82
42 коп.

(5) ☐

5 КАФЕ
ГАСТРОНОМ

(6) ☐

Total out of 25 ☐

Unit 10

1 1 A new camera
2 A Russian camera, 'Zenith'
3 He doesn't want it. He wants a Japanese camera
4 A German one
5 He's in a hurry

(5) ☐

2 1 В 2 Г 3 Б 4 А 5 Б

(5) ☐

3 A — 3
B — 2
C — 3
D — 3
E — 1
F — 4
G — 5

(7) ☐

4

7
11
5
1
3
2
8
10
4
6
12
9

(12) ☐

Your score

■ 5 СТОЛЕ
     ДВА _____ _____ ОДНА ЖЕНЩИНА
     ПО
     СМОТРИТ
     ИДЁТ

                                                                      (5) ☐

Crossword *Across* 1 ПРОСТИТЕ 7 И 10 МНЕ 12 АГА 14 СТОИТ 16 ПУНШ
17 ЭТОТ 19 НО 20 АРЕСТ 22 НО 23 АН 24 РИГЕ 25 ОТ
27 НИЧЕГО 29 ТАК 33 ПО 35 НРАВИТСЯ 36 ДОН 37 НЕ
38 ОЛЯ 40 ГУМ 41 НУ 42 ГУЛЯТЬ 44 ЛЮБЯТ 50 БАР 51 ХОР
52 ЗА 53 ТОМ 54 ЧАСОВ

Down 1 ПОП 2 РЕСТОРАНЕ 3 ОСТ 4 СМОТРЮ 5 ТОВАРИЩ
6 МГУ 7 И 8 НЕ 9 ДЕВЯТЬ 11 НИНА 13 АН 15 ТОННА 16 ПРИ
18 ОНИ 21 СЕГОДНЯ 22 НОТА 26 ДЕВЯТЬ 28 ЧАС 30 КРОЛЬ
31 ДА 32 ИЯЛ 33 ПО 34 ОНА 39 ЛЯ 42 ГАЗ 43 УРА 45 ЮРА
46 БИС 47 ТОВ 48 ИРА 49 ПО 50 БЫ

■ 6

2
1
0
1
2
1
1
2
0
1

                                                                      (10) ☐

                                                          Total out of 44 ☐

Unit 11

Your score

📖 1

TUES	10	11
MON	25	4
SAT	1	7
WED	30	12

(12) ☐

👓 2

9.30–12.00

ЗООПАРК

19.00

23.00

9ое июля

ОБЕД

16.00

07.00–07.30

(8) ☐

📖 3

1	Tuesday	4	13.00
2	Sunday	5	Saturday
3	9.00		

(5) ☐

Total out of 25 ☐

Unit 12

📖 1

1 Coffee and egg
2 Watched the film 'The Black Birch Tree'
3 Physics
4 Mushrooms
5 On a kolkhoz

(5) ☐

📖 2

1   1113–1125
2   1147
3   1223
4   1227
5   1240–1480
6   1326
7   Napoleon
8   1861
9   1914
10 1917
11 1924
12 1953

(12) ☐

Total out of 17 ☐

Crossword   *Across*   1 НЕ   3 МГУ   5 ЛЕВ   8 ЛК   9 МЕТР   11 ЖЕЛЕ   12 ЛЕТ
14 АВИА   17 НИКОН   18 ШЕКСПИР   20 АТА   21 АРАП
23 НИКИТА   26 ПАН   28 ТОВ   30 ПЕТЕРБУРГ   32 МАО   33 БРА
35 И   36 ХАН   37 ИДТИ   38 БКТ

Down   2 ЕЁ   3 МТ   4 УЖЕ   5 ЛЕНИНГРАД   6 ВЕК   7 ФЛОТ
8 ЛЕНА   9 ПА   10 РАСПУТИН   13 ТУЛА   15 ВЕРА   16 ИК
18 ШАПКА   19 РИМ   22 КРЕМ   24 КЛУБ   25 ТОГА   27 НЕВА
29 ВОТ   30 ПУХ   31 БОТ   34 РБ

Unit 13

1
1 The Ukraine hotel
2 The Ukraine hotel
3 Kalinin Prospect
4 Sportivnaya
5 Arbatskaya

(5) ☐

2
3 с пересáдкой (Кúровская)
4 с пересáдкой (Октя́брьская)
5 с пересáдкой (Проспéкт Мáркса)
6 без пересáдки (пять)
7 с пересáдкой (Октя́брьская)
8 с пересáдкой (Проспéкт мúра)
9 без пересáдки (вóсемь)
10 без пересáдки (две)
11 с пересáдкой (Кúевская)
12 без пересáдки (одúннадцать)

(10) ☐

3
1 Ленингрáд
2 6.30 23.55
3 в 8 утрá
4 14р. 20 коп.
5 одúн

(5) ☐

4

						Differences
БАКУ	32.20	42.09	40	2.40	7.80	39 h 29 m
ЕРЕВАН	33.10	51.42	40	2.50	6.90	48 h 52 m
КИЕВ	17.40	11.35	20	1.20	2.60	10 h 15 m
ЛЕНИНГРАД	14.20	5.59	18	1.20	3.80	4 h 39 m
ВЛАДИВОСТОК	93.70	170.00	134	9.55	40.30	160 h 5 m

(10) ☐

Plane arrives at 8.50 in Irkutsk

(1) ☐

Total out of 31 ☐

Unit 14
Comprehension Questions

Moscow 1 Ten million
2 Kalinin Prospect

Leningrad 1 Peterburg
2 Because it has many bridges and canals

Kiev 1 Dnepr (Dnieper)
2 Kreshchatik

Tbilisi 1 Caucasus
2 Pirosmanashvili (Pirosmani)

Riga 1 Latvia
2 The old part

Tashkent 1 Textile factories
2 1·5 million

(12) ☐

📖 1 1 ю́ге
2 за́паде
3 восто́ке
4 ю́го-восто́ке
5 се́веро-за́паде
6 се́вере   (6) ☐

📖 2 1 In Leningrad University
2 Walk along the Nevsky Prospect and look at shop windows.
3 Father was giving a lecture in Kiev at a conference.
4 By night train.
5 That there was an underground in Kiev.
6 Walked in a park by the river and in the evening watched films.
7 Go to Tbilisi.   (7) ☐

📖 3 2 Он хоте́л бы пойти́, но рестора́н сего́дня закры́т.
3 Они́ хоте́ли бы пойти́, но библиоте́ка сего́дня закры́та.
4 Он хоте́л бы пойти́, но кино́ сего́дня закры́то.   (3) ☐

Total out of 28 ☐

Unit 15 2 в 1326 г.
📖 1 3 в 1605 г.
4 в 1703 г.
5 в 1861 г.
6 в 1953 г.   (5) ☐

📖 2 1 Чи́нгиз-хан и монго́льская а́рмия разби́ли славя́нскую
а́рмию.
3 Смерть Бори́са Годуно́ва.
2 Москва́ ста́ла полити́ческим це́нтром Ру́си.
4 Основа́ние Санкт-Петербу́рга.
5 Крестья́нская рефо́рма.
6 Смерть Ста́лина.   (6) ☐

📖 3 1 В 1227г. умер Чингиз-хан.
2 В 1914г. началась Первая Мировая война.
3 В 1697г. Пётр Великий поехал в Голландию.
4 В 1945г. кончилась Вторая Мировая война.
5 В 1480г. кончилось татарское иго.
6 В 1796г. умерла Екатерина Вторая.   (6) ☐

▶ 4

6
2
4
5
9
8
11
10
1
7
3

(11) ☐

▶ 5

1 6ого сентября́
2 Бори́сов Ива́н Никола́евич
3 в сре́ду
4 21ого сентября́
5 Аме́рики

(5) ☐

▶ 6 АЭРОПОРТ ЗАКРЫТ ЕДУ ПОЕЗДОМ БУДУ В МОСКВЕ
10.00 СРЕДА 8 АВГУСТА

(10) ☐

▶ 7

1 Two kopeks.
2 From the hotel room to town numbers.
3 Dial '0', then the number.
4 662

(4) ☐

▶ 8

1 Автомобилист
2 1–5
3 ЦСКА
4 Динамо Москва
5 7
6 Автомобилист
7 В. Белоусов

(7) ☐

Total out of 54 ☐

176

Unit 16

■ ▣ 1
1 Edinburgh, Scotland
2 Wine, champagne, beer, cocktails and cognac.
3 He thinks that Soviet women drink less than British women.
4 He thinks they should be wearing the kilt.
5 That soldiers wear it and it's a national costume, worn on festivals.
6 To the Taganka theatre.   (6) ☐

■ 2
2 ме́ньше (америка́нец)
3 бо́льше (сове́тский/ру́сский)
4 бо́льше (шотла́ндец)   (3) ☐

■ 3
2 пое́дем тролле́йбусом
3 пойти́ в четве́рг
4 хоте́ла бы пойти́
5 бале́т   (4) ☐

■ 4

2
6
4
3
1
5

(6) ☐

Total out of 19 ☐

Unit 17

■ 1
но́вым го́дом
днём рожде́ния
горя́чий приве́т
Поздравля́ю
целу́ю и обнима́ю
всего́ хоро́шего/до́брого   (6) ☐

■ 2
1 Junior chess championship of the world.
2 Graz, Austria.
3 He is also a Russian and he came second, half a point behind, and he is a former champion.
4 Fries-Nielsen.
5 France.
6 Sergei Sukhoruchenkov. 42 h 26 min 28 s.
7 Ramazan Galyaletdinov from Kuibyshev, Sergei Morozov from Leningrad and Alexander Averin from Kuibyshev.   (7) ☐

Total out of 13 ☐   177

Crossword *Across* 1 КОНСТИТУЦИЯ 7 РОД 10 ЮМОР 11 НО 13 ПАПА
14 НО 15 ПРИВЕТ 17 НА 18 ГОДОМ 19 ВЕКЕ 20 ЦК
21 ФИНИШУ 26 ТАТАРКА 27 ЛЕНИН 29 НУ 30 СЫН 31 ХОЛЛ
32 ЦАРЬ 33 ИДУ 34 КЛАСС 37 СТО 39 КАЛИФ 42 СП 44 МАЙ
45 ТОКИО 46 РУСЬ 47 РАЙ 49 СПРИНТ 50 ТЕАТР 51 ДК
52 ПОБЕДА 55 ЛОТО 58 БАХ 60 ПРИ 61 ГОЛ 62 ЗОО 63 НАТО
64 ОСЕНЬЮ 65 АН 66 РИТА
Down 1 КОПЕРНИК 2 СОВЕТСКИЙ 3 ТРЕК 4 ИНТЕРНАЦИОНАЛ
5 ТОН 6 ЯПОНЕЦ 7 РАД 8 ОНО 9 ДОМ 10 ЮРА 12 КАКАО
13 ПО 16 ИВАН 20 ЦК 21 ФИЛИ 22 ИЛЛЮСТРАТОР 23 ИНА
24 ШИРОКИЙ 25 У 26 ТУДА 28 НЬЮ-ЙОРК 35 СТАРТЕР
36 СТАРТ 37 СПОРТ 38 ТАК 40 ФИЛИ 41 ХУЖЕ 43 ГРУППА
44 МУСОР 48 АРБАТ 51 ДАТА 53 БИС 54 ДОН 56 ООН
57 ОНИ 59 ХОР 62 ЗА

Unit 18

📖 👓 **1**

1 High temperature, sore throat, slight headache, no appetite.
2 That it's a cold and that he should have tea with lemon.
3 Looks at his throat and takes his temperature. Writes out a prescription.
4 Tablets three times a day, rest in bed.   (4) ☐

📖 **2**

5	4
4	2
1	3
2	5
3	1

(10) ☐

📖 **3**

5
1
4
7
3
2
6

(7) ☐

Total out of 21 ☐

178

Unit 19

1 Иванóв
Михаи́л Бори́сович
16ого ма́рта 1964
Ки́ев
Ру́сский
Ерева́нская ул. 6 кв. 18
М.Б. Иванóв
16ое ию́ля   (8) ☐

2
1 Boring
2 The weather was hot.
3 To the lake.
4 It was forbidden and she didn't have a costume.
5 She was watching Misha.
6 Misha didn't have any money.
7 In the cinema.
8 In the police station.
9 Five roubles.
10 That he should pay a fine of three roubles and that the next time...   (10) ☐

3 СССР
МОСКВА
Ереванская ул.6 кв. 18
Иванову М.Б.   (4) ☐

Total out of 22   ☐

Unit 20

1

4					11		1
6					10		2
5	7	8	9		12		3

(12) ☐

2 a

5
3
1
2
4

(5) ☐

b
(i) Дóброе у́тро
Здра́вствуйте/пожива́ете   (3) ☐

(ii) Прия́тного аппети́та
Спаси́бо   (2) ☐

(iii) Всегó
Всегó хорóшего/лу́чшего   (2) ☐

(iv) Спокóйной нóчи
Спокóйной нóчи   (2) ☐

179

Crossword

Across 1 АПТЕКА 5 ВРАЧ 8 ХОРОШО 13 ДВЕ 14 МИСС
15 ЛИМОН 17 МОСТ 18 ГРИПП 19 ЕГИП 21 ЛЕЖАТЬ 22 МЫ
23 РИС 25 ИДИОТ 26 АТА 28 НЕОН 30 ПРОСТУДА 34 ЛЕНИН
35 ИМЯ 36 ИДТИ 38 ПОРА 39 НО 40 СТЕНД 42 ПОКА
44 ОПТИК 45 ОН 47 ТУТ 48 ТАКСИ 51 ОПУС 54 ОРДЕН
55 РЕЦЕПТ 58 ПОТЕРЯЛА 60 АМПЕР 64 АЦИ 65 ПРИ 67 БАКУ
68 ПИОНЕР 69 КЛИМАТ 70 ФОТО 71 СОЧИ 72 ИДЕТ 74 АО
76 ТРИ 79 ДА 80 ТОВ 81 ИТ 82 ЯР 83 АМИН 86 НОРМА 88 ЗА
89 ПОЛИКЛИНИКА 91 ЗОЯ 92 МИР 93 ХАН 96 НО 98 ТВИСТ
100 НА 101 ТЕМПЕРАТУРА

Down 1 АДМИНИСТРАЦИЯ 2 ТЕРМОМЕТР 3 КИПР
4 АСПИРИН 5 ВСЕ 6 АИ 7 ЧМПИ 8 ХОЛОДНО 9 РОЖА
10 ШОТА 11 ОС 12 СТЫДНО 16 НЕТ 17 МАТЕРИ 18 ГДЕ
20 ИДТИ 24 СО 27 КИНО 29 НЯ 30 ПЕД 31 СТОИТ 32 У ВАС
33 АППЕТИТА 34 ЛОТО 37 ДП 41 ТУДА 43 КА 46 НРАВИТСЯ
48 ТЕ 49 СПАРТАК 50 ГОРОД 52 ПРА 53 СЛУЧИЛОСЬ
56 ЦЕНА 57 МИЛИЦИЯ 58 ПП 59 ЯКОВ 61 МИ 62 ПО 63 РЕ
65 ЦК 71 СОМ 73 ДРАМА 75 ОНИ 77 РОЛЬ 78 ЗЕНИТ 80 ТРАТ
83 АП 84 МОРЕ 85 ИЛ 86 НИНУ 87 АЗИЯ 88 ЗОН 90 ДВА
91 ЗОЯ 94 АП 95 НЕ 97 ОР 99 ТО

▌3

a	пло́хо
b	неё
c	хо́лодно
d	апте́ку
e	медикаме́нты

(5) ☐

▌4

f
g
e
a
c
b
h
j
d
i

(10) ☐

Total out of 41 ☐

Vocabulary

This is a combined vocabulary and index, in that it includes not only the meaning of the words in the context in which they appear in the course, but also the number of the unit in which they first occur (in parentheses). Not all of the words in the course are included in the vocabulary, and not all of the words in the vocabulary will be of critical importance to the beginner in Russian. Pronouns and numerals have been excluded, as they appear elsewhere, and many of the words which appear only in crosswords have been left out, and may be checked in the keys to the crosswords. Some cognates (words like English words) have also been omitted.

The meanings given are those which apply in the context of the course. Adjectives are given with masculine, feminine and neuter endings and an underlining means that this is the form in which the word first occurs in the course.

trans.	=	transliteration
к.	=	crossword
n.	=	noun
adj.	=	adjective

Vocabulary

A

а (2)	*but, and*
а́виа/авиапо́чта (1)	*airmail*
австри́йский (17)	*Austrian*
авто́бус (3)	*bus*
автома́т (6)	*machine (vending);*
телефон-автомат	*telephone booth*
актри́са (10)	*actress*
амазо́нка (20) (к.)	*Amazon (woman warrior)*
англи́йский (7)	*English*
англича́нин (-ка) (7)	*Englishman (woman)*
анке́та (19)	*questionnaire*
антреко́т (9)	*entrecote*
аппара́т (1)	*camera*
апре́ль (11)	*April*
апте́ка (2)	*chemist*
а́рмия (12)	*army*
архитекту́ра (14)	*architecture*
аспиранту́ра (15)	*post-graduate course*
африка́нец, африка́нка (7)	*African (n.)*
африка́нский (7)	*African (adj.)*

Б

балко́н (4)	*balcony*
бассе́йн (19)	*swimming pool*
бежа́ть (10)	*run*
без (13) (+gen.)	*without*
бе́лый (-ая, -ое, -ые) (9)	*white*
берёза (12)	*birch tree*
беспла́тно (15)	*free*
библиоте́ка (12)	*library*
биле́т (4)	*ticket*
бифште́кс (5)	*beefsteak, hamburger*
бланк (4)	*form*
блю́до/-а/ (9)	*dish, course*
боле́ть, заболе́ть (15)	*to be ill, to fall ill*
больни́ца (15)	*hospital*
бо́льно, боли́т (18)	*bad (hurting)*
больно́й (19)	*patient*
бо́льше (16)	*more, bigger*
большо́й (-ое, -ая) (5)	*large, big*
борщ (5)	*beetroot soup*
бракосочета́ние (19)	*wedding, marriage*
брат (12)	*brother*
бу́ду see быть (11)	*will*
бу́дущий (-ая, -ее, -ие) (14)	*future*

(continued)

бульва́р (5)	*boulevard*
бульо́н (3)	*clear soup*
бума́жник (19)	*wallet*
буфе́т (3)	*buffet*
бы (14)	*[indicates would, might]*
был (-á) (12)	*was*
быть	*to be*
бу́ду, бу́дешь, бу́дем, бу́дете, бу́дут (11)	*(future tense)*
бюро́ (3)	*office*

B

в (2)	*in (+loc.), into (+acc.)*
ваго́н-рестора́н (13)	*restaurant car*
вальс (8)	*waltz*
валю́та (19)	*hard currency (dollars, pounds, marks, etc.)*
вам (6)	*to you, for you (dat. of* вы*)*
вас (2)	*you (acc. of* вы*)*
ваш (-а, -е, -и) (6)	*your*
ведь (19)	*indeed*
век (12) (к.)	*century*
вели́кий (-ая, -ое, -ие) (12)	*great*
велого́нка (17)	*bicycle race*
велосипе́д (17)	*bicycle*
весна́, весно́й (11)	*spring, in spring*
весь (вся, всё, все) (14)	*all, whole*
ветчина́ (9)	*ham*
ве́чер (8)	*evening*
ве́чером (10)	*in the evening*
вече́рний (-яя, -ее, -ие) (8)	*evening (adj.)*
взлёт (11)	*take-off*
взять (10)	*to take*
возьми́, возьми́те (6)	*take! (imperative)*
ви́деть, уви́деть (14)	*to see, to spot*
вино́ (1)	*wine*
витри́на (14)	*shop window*
вкус (16)	*taste*
вку́сный (9)	*tasty*
вку́сно	*tasty (adverb)*
вода́ (2)	*water*
во́здух (19)	*air*
война́ (12)	*war*
вокза́л (13)	*station (terminal)*
воскресе́ние (11)	*Resurrection*
воскресе́нье (11)	*Sunday*
восста́ние (11)	*uprising*

восто́к (14)	east
восто́чный (-ая, -ое, -ые) (14)	east (adj.)
вот (2)	here is
врач (18)	doctor
вре́мя (8)	time
все (9)	everyone
всегда́ (3) (trans.) (17)	always
всё (10)	everything
встава́ть (11) (встать)	to get up
встреча́ться, встре́титься (17)	to meet
вто́рник (11)	Tuesday
второ́й (-а́я, -о́е, -ы́е) (8)	second
вход (3)	entrance
входи́ть (4)	to enter
вчера́ (12)	yesterday
выпи́сывать, вы́писать (9)	to write out
высо́кий (-ая, -ое, -ие) (14)	high
выступа́ть, вы́ступить (12)	to make a speech
вы́сший (-ая, -ее, -ие) (15)	higher (education, etc.)
вы́ход (4)	exit
выходи́ть (4)	to go out
выходно́й (11)	day off

Г

газе́та (4)	newspaper
газиро́ванная (trans.) вода́ (2)	carbonated, fizzy water
газо́н (4)	lawn, grass
гастроно́м (10)	delicatessen; grocers
где (2) (trans.) (12)	where
гидроста́нция (13)	hydro-electric power station
гла́вный (-ая, -ое, -ые) (10)	main
глазно́й (-о́е, -а́я, -ы́е) (18)	eye (adj.)
говори́ть (7)	to speak
год (4)	year
годо́вщина (17)	anniversary
голова́ (18)	head
голубо́й (-а́я, -о́е, -ы́е) (14)	pale blue
го́нки (17)	races
го́рло (18)	throat
го́род (4)	city, town
городско́й (-а́я, -о́е, -и́е) (18)	municipal, urban
горя́чий (-яя, -ее, -ие) (17)	hot
гостеприи́мство (16)	hospitality
гости́ница (10)	hotel
госуда́рственный (8)	state
гото́в (-а, -о, -ы) (9)	ready

граждани́н (-ка) (7)	citizen
гражда́нский (-ая, -ое, -ие) (12)	civil, civic
гриб (4)	mushroom
грипп (18)	influenza
грузи́н, грузи́нка (7)	Georgian (n.)
грузи́нский (-ая, -ое, -ие) (7)	Georgian (adj.)
гуля́ть, погуля́ть (8)	to stroll, to have a stroll

Д

да (1)	yes
дава́й (-те)	let's
дава́ть (6)	to give
дать, да́йте (10)	give!
да́ча (19)	summer house, country house
дверь (-и) (13)	door
дворе́ц (5)	palace
де́вочка (6)	(little) girl
де́вушка (6)	(unmarried) girl
дегуста́ция (9)	tasting
дежу́рная (18)	woman on duty
дека́брь (11)	December
дела́ (2)	things, affairs
де́лать (10)	to do, to make
демонстра́ция (5)	demonstration
день (11)	day
днём	in the afternoon
де́ньги (19)	money
де́ти (7)	children
де́тский сад (15)	kindergarten
диссерта́ция (15)	dissertation
для (5)	for
до (9)	up to
до свида́ния (1) (trans.) (10)	goodbye
до́брый (-ая, -ое, -ые) (16)	kind, good
до́лжен (должна́, должно́, должны́) (18)	ought
дом/до́ма/ (2)	house, at home
до́рого (9)	dear
дорого́й (-а́я, -о́е, -и́е) (15)	dear
друг (plur. друзья́) (7)	friend
друго́й (-а́я, -о́е, -и́е) (14)	another
ду́мать (12)	to think
душа́ (18)	soul
ду́шно (19)	stuffy

Е

еди́ный (6)	single, one
е́сли (15)	if
есть (6)	there is, is

183

éхать, поéхать, éздить (13) — to go (by vehicle)
ещё (9) — move, still

Ж

жáловаться (19) — complain
жáреный (9) — roast, grilled, fried
жáрко (18) — hot
желáть (17) — to wish
желé (9) — jelly
женá — wife
жéнский (-ая, -ое, -ие) (5) — woman's, female
жéнщина (5) — woman
жёсткий (-ая, -ое, -ие) (13) — hard
жить (12) — to live

З

за (10) (к.) — for
зáвтра (3) (trans.) (10) — tomorrow
зáвтрак (11) — breakfast, lunch
зáвтракать, позáвтракать (12) — to have breakfast, lunch
заказáть, (закáзывать) (18) — to order
закрывáть, закры́ть (13) — to close
закры́т (-а, -о, -ы) (3) (trans.) (8) — closed
закýска (-и) (9) — hors-d'oeuvre (-s) snack
зал (13) — hall
замечáтельно (10) — splendid, wonderful
занимáть, заня́ть (17) — to occupy
занимáться, заня́ться (15) — to study
зáнят (-а, -ы) (9) — occupied
зáпад (12) — west
зáпадный (14) — western
заря́дка (6) — exercises
затéм (15) — next
звать (7) — to call
звони́ть (15) позвони́ть — to ring (telephone)
здáние (14) — building
здесь (2) (trans.) (4) — here
здорóв (-а, -о, -ы) (17) — well, healthy
здорóвье (9) — health
здрáвствуйте (1) (trans.) (7) — hello
зелёный (-ая, -ое, -ые) (14) — green
зимá (11) — winter
зимóй (11) — in winter

знакóмиться, познакóмиться (7) — to get to know someone
знакóмый (-ая, -ое, -ые) (7) — acquaintance
знамени́тый (-ая, -ое, -ые) (14) — well-known, famous
знать (14) — to know
знáчит — it means
зовýт (как вас зовýт?) (2) (from звать) — (what is your name?)
зоопáрк (2) — zoo
зубнóй (-áя, -óе, -ы́е) (18) — dental

И

и (1) — and
и́го (12) — yolk
игрáть, сыгрáть (7) — to play
идёт (что идёт?) (5) — is going (on) (what's on?)
идти́ (5) — to go
из (10) (к.) — out of (+gen.)
извéстия (4) — news
извини́те! (3) — excuse me!
икрá (9) — caviar
и́ли (16) — or
и́мя (7) — first name
индéйка (9) — turkey
иногдá (16) — sometimes
интернáт (-ы) (15) — boarding school
истори́ческий (10) — historical
истóрия (12) — history
и́юль (11) — July
и́юнь (11) — June

К

кавкáзский (-ая, -ое, -ие) (14) — Caucasian
кáждый (12) — each
казáться, показáться (16) — to seem
кáжется (16) — it seems
как (2) — how
какóй (-áя, -óе, -и́е) (11) — what kind of
карти́на (-ы) (14) — picture
картóфельный (9) — potato
кáсса (1) — cash-desk, ticket desk
катáние на конькáх (3) — skating
на лы́жах — skiing
кáтер (13) — cutter, motor launch (hydrofoil)
кварти́ра (2) — flat, apartment
ки́евский (-ая, -ое, -ие) (12) — Kiev (adj.)

184

кино́ (2)	cinema
кита́ец, китая́нка (7)	Chinese (n.)
кита́йский (7)	Chinese (adj.)
кли́мат (3)	climate, weather
кни́га (12)	book
князь (12)	prince
'Князь И́горь'	Prince Igor
когда́ (8) (3) (trans.)	when
когда́-то (15)	at one time
колле́га (masc.) (7)	colleague
колхо́з (12)	collective farm
колхо́зный	collective farm (adj.)
комбина́т (18)	combine
коме́та (1)	comet
комите́т (12) (к.)	committee
ко́мната (8)	room
компо́т (9)	stewed fruit
комсомо́лец (15)	young communist league member
коне́чно (15)	of course
конча́ть, ко́нчить, конча́ться (15)	finish
кооперати́вный (-ая, -ое, -ые) (19)	cooperative (adj.)
копе́йка (6)	kopek
коридо́р (8)	corridor
ко́смос (9)	space
костю́м (3)	suit
котле́та (-ы) (9)	cutlet
кото́рый (-ая, -ое, -ые) (8)	which
краси́вый (5)	beautiful
кра́сный (-ая, -ое, -ые) (5)	red
крем (12) (к.)	cream
кре́пко (12)	firmly
крестья́нин, крестья́нка, крестья́не (12)	peasant
крестья́нский (-ая, -ое, -ие) (12)	peasant (adj.)
кроль (10) (к.)	crawl (swimming)
кто (1)	who
кукуру́за (9)	sweet corn
купа́льный (19)	swimming
купа́ться, искупа́ться (19)	to bathe
купи́ть, покупа́ть (10)	to buy
кури́ть (4)	to smoke
ку́рица, ку́ра (9)	chicken
куро́рт (-ы) (18)	resort
куря́щий (5)	smoking
ку́шать (9)	to eat

Л

ла́дно (7)	O.K., fine
лежа́ть (15)	to lie
ле́кция (5)	lecture
ле́то (11)	summer
ле́том	in summer
ли́га (15)	league
лимо́нный (-ая, -ое, -ые) (9)	lemon (adj.)
ли́шний (16)	extra, spare
лу́чше (16)	better
люби́ть (8)	to love
любо́вь (fem.)	love
лю́ди	people

М

магази́н (10)	shop
май (4)	May
ма́ленький (-ая, -ое, -ие)	small
ма́рка (1)	stamp, model
март (11)	March
маршру́тный (-ая, -ое, -ые) (13)	fixed route (taxi)
ма́сло (9)	butter
маши́на (5)	car
междунаро́дный (-ая, -ое, -ые) (17)	international
ме́лочь (6)	small change
ме́ньше (16)	less
ме́сто (4)	place, seat
ме́сяц (6)	month
милиционе́р (plur. -ы) (16)	policeman
мили́ция (19)	police station
ми́лый (-ая, -ое, -ые) (11)	kind, nice
министе́рство (9)	ministry
мир (2)	peace, world
мирово́й (-ая, -ое, -ы́е) (12)	world (adj.)
мно́го (14)	many, a lot
мо́жет быть (16)	perhaps
мо́жно (5)	one may
мой, моя́, моё, мои́ (7)	my
молодо́й (19)	young
монасты́рь (10)	monastery
монго́льский (-ая, -ое, -ие) (12)	Mongol
моне́та (6)	coin
мо́ре (14)	sea
моро́женое (9)	ice-cream
москви́ч (5)	Muscovite (n.)
моско́вский (-ая, -ое, -ие) (10)	Muscovite (adj.)
мост (14)	bridge
мото́р (-ы) (6) (к.)	engine
муж (17)	husband

мужско́й (-а́я) (5)	man's (gentleman's)
мужчи́на (5)	man
музе́й (10)	museum, art gallery
му́сор (к.) (17)	rubbish
мы (8)	we
мя́гкий (-ая, -ое, -ие) (13)	soft
мясно́й (9)	meat (adj.)
мя́со (9)	meat (n.)

Н

на (2)	on (+loc.), onto (+acc.)
набира́ть, набра́ть (15)	to dial
на́до (11)	it is necessary
наза́д (тому́ наза́д) (15)	ago
называ́ть, назва́ть (14)	to call
нале́во (3)	to the left
напи́тки (9)	drinks
напра́во (3)	to the right
наприме́р (14)	for example
наро́дный (8)	folk
натура́льный (5)	natural
нау́ка (15)	science
находи́ть, найти́ (19)	to find
находи́ться (14)	to be situated
национа́льность (19)	nationality
национа́льный (-ая, -ое, -ые) (16)	national
начина́ться, начина́ть, нача́ть (12)	to begin
наш (7)	our
не (1)	not
небольшо́й (-а́я, -о́е, -и́е) (13)	small
невку́сный (9)	not tasty
невозмо́жно (19)	impossible
недалеко́ (19)	not far
неде́ля (15)	week
некуря́щий (5)	non-smoking
нельзя́ (4)	it is forbidden
неме́цкий (10)	German
нео́н (20) (к.)	neon
не́сколько (12)	some
нет (1)	no
неудовлетвори́тельно (15)	unsatisfactory
нехорошо́ (1)	bad
никогда́ (16)	never
ничего́ (2) (trans.) (10)	never mind, nothing, it's nothing, all right
но (3)	but
новобра́чный новобра́чная новобра́чные (19)	newly-wed
но́вости (8)	news

но́вый (-ая, -ое) (8)	new
носи́ть, нести́ (16)	to carry
но́та (10) (к.)	a note
ночно́й (-а́я, -о́е, -ы́е) (14)	night (adj.)
ночь (11)	night (n.)
но́чью (11)	at night
ноя́брь (11)	November
нра́вится, понра́виться (8)	to like
ну (ну да) (7)	well
ну́жен (-на́, -но, -ны́) (10)	necessary
ну́жный (15)	necessary

О

о, об (10)	about (+loc.)
обе́д (11)	lunch
обе́дать, пообе́дать (11)	to have lunch
обе́денный (11)	lunch (adj.)
обнима́ть, обня́ть (17)	to embrace
обслу́живание (6)	service
обстре́л (артобстре́л) (12)	bombardment
одна́жды (12)	one day, once upon a time, once
о́зеро (19)	lake
окно́ (14)	window
о́коло (14)	about (+gen.)
оконча́ние (8)	the end
октябрёнок (15)	child member of the 'October' organisation
октя́брь (11)	October
октя́брьский (12)	October (adj.)
опа́здывать, опозда́ть (9)	to be late
опя́ть (18)	again
о́рден (4)	order
освобожде́ние (12)	liberation
о́сень (11)	autumn
о́сенью	in autumn
осётр (9)	sturgeon
основа́ние (12)	foundation
остано́вка (13)	stop
осторо́жно (13)	careful
от (10) (к.)	from (+да)
о́тдых (18)	rest
отдыха́ть (18)	to rest
оте́ц	father
оте́чественный (-ая, -ое, -ые) (12)	patriotic
откры́т (3) (trans.) (5)	open
откры́тка (5)	post-card
откры́ть	to open
отку́да (16)	from whence
отли́чно (15)	excellent
отправи́тель (19)	sender

отправле́ние (13)	departure
отту́да (14)	from there
отходи́ть (13)	to go away from
о́тчество (7)	patronymic
отъе́зд (11)	departure
официа́нтка (9)	waitress
о́чень (2) (trans.) (8)	very
о́чередь (9)	queue
о́чи (14)	eyes
очко́, очки́ (15)	point (s)

П

пальто́ (20) (к.)	coat
парте́р (4)	stalls
пе́рвенство (17)	championship
пе́рвый (-ая, -ое, -ые) (4)	first
передава́ть, переда́ть (8)	to pass, transmit
переда́ча	transmission, programme
перезва́нивать, перезвони́ть (6)	to phone again
переры́в (11)	intermission, break
переса́дка (13)	change
перехо́д (3)	crossing
переходи́ть (5)	to cross
пи́во (2)	beer
пионе́р (15)	pioneer
писа́ть, написа́ть (пиши́) (10)	to write
письмо́ (12)	letter
пить (9)	to drink
пла́вать (19)	to swim
пла́вки (19)	swimming trunks
плати́ть (6)	pay
пло́хо (15) (2) (trans.)	badly
пло́щадь (5)	square
пляж (14)	beach
по (8)	along (+dat.)
по-англи́йски (8)	in English
по-мо́ему (8)	in my opinion
по-тво́ему по-ва́шему и т.д.}	in your opinion etc.
побе́да (17)	victory
побежда́ть, победи́ть (17)	to win, defeat
пого́да (12)	weather
по́дпись (19)	signature
поликли́ника (18)	polyclinic
полчаса́ (18)	half an hour
по́люс (к.)	pole
помога́ть, помо́чь (помоги́те!) (18)	to help (help!)
понеде́льник (11)	Monday

понима́ть, поня́ть (19)	to understand
поня́тно (18)	understood
пора́ (20) (к.)	it's time
по́сле (11)	after (+gen.)
поступа́ть, поступи́ть (15)	to start (school, etc.)
пото́м (12)	afterwards
потому́ что (8)	because
почему́ (8)	why
по́чта (5)	post office
по́эзия (8)	poetry
пра́вда (2)	truth
пра́здник	holiday, feast day
предпочита́ть (16)	prefer
представля́ть, предста́вить (7)	present
при (к.) (17)	in the time of, attached to (+loc.)
прибы́тие (13)	arrival
приве́т (7)	greetings
приезжа́ть (11)	to arrive
приём (9)	reception
принима́ть (18)	take
приходи́ть, придти́ (10)	to arrive
прия́тно (2) (trans.) (16)	it's a pleasure
проводни́к, проводни́ца (13)	attendant (on train)
пропи́ска (19)	registration, residence permit
про́пуск (4)	pass
пропуска́ть, пропусти́ть (13)	to let through
проси́ть, попроси́ть (15)	to ask
прости́ть, прости́те (3)	to excuse, excuse me
просту́да (18)	cold
профсою́з (3)	trade union
проходи́ть, пройти́, пройдёмте (19)	to go through, to pass, go along to
про́шлый (-ая, -ое, -ые) (12)	past (adj.)
пря́мо (3)	straight (adv.)
прямо́й (-а́я, -о́е, -ы́е) (14)	straight (adj.)
пух (12) (к.)	fluff
пье́са (16)	play
пя́тница (11)	Friday
пя́тый (-ая, -ое, -ые) (11)	fifth

Р

рабо́та (14)	work
ра рабо́те	at work
рабо́тать (9)	to work
рад (2) (trans.) (10)	glad, pleased
раз (6)	once, one (time)

187

разбива́ть, разби́ть (12)	smash
разгова́ривать (19)	to converse
разреша́ть (7)	to allow
разреша́ется (19)	it is allowed
рай (к.) (17)	paradise
райо́н (14)	region
райо́нный (-ая, -ое, -ые) (18)	regional
раке́та (13)	rocket
ра́но (13)	early
ра́ньше (14)	sooner
расписа́ние (13)	timetable
распи́сываться, расписа́ться (19)	to sign
ре́дко (16)	rarely
результа́т (15)	result
река́ (14)	river
ремо́нт (на ремо́нте)	repair (under repair)
респу́блика (14)	republic
рестора́н (1)	restaurant
рефо́рма (12)	reform
реце́пт (18)	prescription
речно́й (-а́я, -о́е, -ы́е) (13)	river (adj.)
рис (20) к.	rice
род (17) к.	kind or sort
ро́жа (20) к.	snout, ugly mug
рожде́ние (17)	birth
роль (10)	role, part
ры́ба (9)	fish
ры́нок (12)	market
ряд (4)	row
ря́дом (19)	alongside

С

с (9)	with, from
сад (14)	garden
сади́ться (9)	to sit down or to get on (a bus)
сала́т (9)	salad
самолёт (4)	aeroplane
санита́рный день (11)	cleaning day
сбо́рная кома́нда (8)	representative (i.e. international) team
сва́дьба (9)	wedding
све́жий (-ая, -ое, -ие) (19)	fresh
свобо́ден (-на, -но, -ны) (9)	free
сдава́ть, сдать экза́мены (12)	to pass examinations
себе́, себя́ (18)	oneself
се́вер (14)	north
се́верный (-ая, -ое, -ые)	northern

се́веро-восто́к (14)	north-east
се́веро-за́пад (14)	north-west
сего́дня (3)	today
сейча́с (3) (5)	immediately
селёдка (9)	herring
семина́ры (15)	seminars
сентя́брь (11)	September
сиде́ть (12)	to sit
симпати́чный (15)	sympathetic
си́ний (-яя, -ее, -ие) (14)	deep blue
сказа́ть (скажи́те) (7)	to say (tell me)
ско́лько (6)	how much, how many
скоре́е (15)	as soon (quickly) as possible
ску́чно (18)	boring
сла́ва (17)	glory
славя́нский (-ая, -ое, -ие) (12)	slavonic
сла́дкий (-ая, -ое, -ие) (9)	sweet
сле́дующий (-ая, -ее, -ие) (13)	following
случи́лось (19)	happened
слу́шать (6)	to listen
смерть (12)	death
смотре́ть, посмотре́ть (8)	to watch, look
собо́р (10)	cathedral
совсе́м (18)	quite, completely
совхо́з (12)	state farm
согла́сен (-на, -но, -ны) (16)	agreed
соединя́ться, соедини́ться (17)	to unite
сожале́ние (16)	regret, pity
к сожале́нию	unfortunately
сок (9)	juice
сою́з (3)	union
спаси́бо (1)	thank you
спать (14)	to sleep
спекта́кль (-и) (11)	play, performance
спи́чки (9)	matches
споко́йный (-ая, -ое, -ые) (17)	peaceful, calm
спра́вочное бюро́ (13)	inquiry office
спу́тник (6)	satellite
среда́ (11)	Wednesday
сре́дняя шко́ла (15)	secondary (middle) school
станови́ться, стать (12)	to become
ста́нция (13)	station
ста́рый (-ая, -ое, -ые) (14)	old
стенд (20) (к.)	stand (in an exhibition)
стиль (19)	style
сто́ить (6)	to cost
стол (7)	table

столи́ца (14)	*capital city*
столо́вая (12)	*dining room, canteen*
сторона́ (12)	*side*
стоя́нка (3)	*stand (of taxis)*
стоя́ть (14)	*to stand*
страна́ (15)	*country, land*
стрела́ (13)	*arrow*
сты́дно (18)	*shameful*
как вам не сты́дно!	*you ought to be ashamed!*
суббо́та (11)	*Saturday*
схе́ма (10)	*plan*
счёт (9)	*bill*
Съезд (5)	*congress*
сын (17)	*son*
сюда́ (19)	*(to) here*

Т

так (9)	*so, thus*
так как (19)	*since*
та́кже (17)	*also*
тало́н (6)	*coupon*
там (3)	*there*
танцева́ть, потанцева́ть (8)	*to dance*
тари́фы (13)	*prices, tariffs*
тата́рин (тата́рка, тата́ры) (17)	*Tatar (n.)*
тата́рский (-ая, -ое, -ие) (12)	*Tatar (adj.)*
тебе́, тебя́ (7)	*you (dative and genitive)*
телеви́дение (8)	*television*
телеви́зор (8)	*television (set)*
телефо́н-автома́т (3)	*public telephone*
тепе́рь (15)	*now*
тепло́ (18)	*warm*
теря́ть, потеря́ть (19)	*to lose*
типи́чный (14)	*typical*
тира́ж (8)	*draw*
ти́хо (19)	*quietly*
то (10)	*that one*
това́рищ (7)	*comrade*
тогда́ (13)	*then*
то-есть (16)	*that is*
то́же (14)	*also*
то́лстый (-ая, -ое, -ые) (14)	*fat, stout*
то́лько (9)	*only*
тон (10) (к.)	*tone (in music)*
то́нна (10) (к.)	*ton*
тот (6)	*that*
трамва́й (6)	*tram*
трек (17) (к.)	*track (athletic)*

тре́тий (-ья, -ье, -ьи) (8)	*third*
труд (17)	*labour*
тру́дно (10)	*difficult*
туда́ (6)	*(to) there*

У

у (6)	*(+gen.) by, with, of etc.*
удовлетвори́тельно (15)	*satisfactory, satisfactorily*
ужа́сный (14)	*awful, terrible*
уже́ (12) (к.)	*already*
у́жин (11)	*supper*
у́жинать, поу́жинать (11)	*to have supper*
узбе́к (3)	*Uzbek (n.)*
узбе́кский (7)	*Uzbek (adj.)*
у́зкий (-ая, -ое, -ие) (14)	*narrow*
украи́нец -ка (7)	*Ukrainian (n.)*
украи́нский (-ая, -ое, -ие)	*Ukrainian (adj.)*
у́лица (10)	*street*
умира́ть, умере́ть (15)	*to die*
уника́льный (-ая, -ое, -ые)	*unique*
ура́ (10) (к.)	*hurray*
успе́х (17)	*success*
у́тренний (-яя, -ее, -ие) (6)	*morning (adj.)*
у́тро (11)	*morning (n.)*
у́тром	*in the morning*
учени́к, учени́ца (15)	*pupil*
учёт (9)	*accounting, stock-taking*
учи́ться (12)	*to study*

Ф

фами́лия (7)	*surname*
февра́ль (11)	*February*
фи́зика (12)	*Physics*
физиотерапевти́ческий (-ая, -ое, -ие) (18)	*physiotherapy (adj.)*
филе́ (9)	*fillet*
флот (4)	*fleet*
фото-аппара́т (3)	*camera*
фру́кты (9)	*fruit*

Х

хлеб (9)	*bread*
ходи́ть (4)	*to go on foot*
хозя́йство (12)	*farm*
холл, мю́зик-холл (17) (к.)	*hall, music hall*
хо́лодно (18)	*cold*
хор (8)	*choir*
хорошо́ (1)	*good, well*
хоте́ть (9)	*to want, to like*
худо́жник (14)	*artist, painter*
ху́же (16)	*worse*

Ц

царь (5)	*tsar, king*
цветы́ (5)	*flowers*
целова́ть, поцелова́ть (17)	*to kiss*
цена́ (20)	*price*
центр (5)	*centre*
цирк (5)	*circus*

Ч

чай (5)	*tea*
час (8)	*hour*
ча́сто (12)	*often*
часы́ (10)	*watch, clock*
чек (6)	*cheque*
челове́к (14)	*person, man*
чем (16)	*than*
че́рез (18)	*in, across*
че́стный (-ая, -ое, -ые) (19)	*honest*
четве́рг (11)	*Thursday*
четвёртый (-ая, -ое, -ые) (8)	*fourth*
чёрный (-ая, -ое, -ые) (9)	*black*
число́ (11)	*date*
чита́ть (8)	*to read*
что (1)	*what*
что́бы (15)	*in order that, in order to*
что́-нибудь (18)	*something, anything*
чу́вствовать себя́ (18)	*to feel*
чуде́сный (-ая, -ое, -ые) (14)	*wonderful*

Ш

шампа́нское (5)	*champagne*
ша́пка (5)	*cap*
ша́хматы (17)	*chess*
шашлы́к (5)	*shashlyk (kebab)*
шашлы́чная	*shashlyk restaurant*
широ́кий (-ая, -ое, -ие) (14)	*wide, broad*
шко́ла (15)	*school*
шоссе́ (5)	*chaussée*
шотла́ндский (16)	*Scottish*
шпро́ты (9)	*sprats*
штраф (19)	*fine (penalty)*

Щ

щи (5)	*cabbage soup*

Э

электри́чество (5)	*electricity*
эне́ргия (4)	*energy*
эта́ж (5)	*floor, storey*
э́то (1) trans. (5)	*this is*

Ю

ю́бка (16)	*skirt*
юг (14)	*south*
юго-восто́к (14)	*south-east*
юго-за́пад (14)	*south-west*
ю́ный (-ая, -ое, -ые)	*young*

Я

язы́к (16)	*language, tongue*
яи́чница (9)	*egg dish*
яйцо́ (9)	*egg*
янва́рь (11)	*January*
япо́нец, япо́нка (7)	*Japanese (n.)*
япо́нский (-ая, -ое, -ие) (7)	*Japanese (adj.)*
я́сли (15)	*crèche, day nursery*

Suggested Reading

BERGER, J. *Art and revolution: Ernest Neizvestny and the role of the artist in the USSR* Weidenfeld and Nicolson, 1969.

CHERNOV, V. *Moscow: a short guide* Central Books, 1977.

DAVIES, R. W. and SHAW, D. J. B. eds. *The Soviet Union* Allen and Unwin, cased and paperback 1978.

FEIFER, G. *Moscow farewell* J. Cape, 1976; Quartet, 1978.

FEIFER, G. *Russia close-up* J. Cape, 1973.

GERHART, G. *The Russian's world: life and language* N.Y.: Harcourt, Brace, Jovanovich, 1974.

KAISER, R. G. *Russia: the people and the power* Secker and Warburg, 1976; Penguin Books, 1977.

LEYDA, J. *Kino: a history of the Russian and Soviet film* Allen and Unwin, n.e. 1973.

LOUIS, V. and J. *The complete guide to the Soviet Union* M. Joseph, 1976.

MACLEAN, FITZROY *Holy Russia* Weidenfeld and Nicolson, 1978.

MILLER, A. and MORATH, I. *In Russia* Secker and Warburg, 1969.

MILLER, W. *Russians as people* Phoenix House, 1960, op.

MILLER, W. *Who are the Russians? A history of the Russian people* Faber, 1973.

NETTL, J. P. *The Soviet achievement* Thames and Hudson, 1967.

PARKER, W. H. *The Russians* (How they live and work) David and Charles, 1973.

SMITH, D. *Guide to Moscow* J. Cape, 1976.

SMITH, H. *The Russians* Times Books, 1976; Sphere, 1977.

SWAN, A. J. *Russian music and its sources in chant and folk-song* J. Baker, 1973.

WARRACK, J. *Tchaikovsky* H. Hamilton, 1973.

YEVTUSHENKO, Y. *The face behind the face* M. Boyars, 1979.

Message from Moscow, by an observer J. Cape, 1969.

Further information can be obtained from:
The Great Britain–USSR Association,
14 Grosvenor Place London SW1.

Acknowledgements

I wish to thank the following for their help in constructing this course: Terry Doyle, Vaughan James and Tanya Chambers for reading the drafts of the book and for their practical help in constructing the course as a whole; Doreen Waller did most of the typing; Rima Greenhill helped at one stage when the pressure was on; Mary Sprent and Chris Serle, who acted as informed guinea-pigs, as well as providing practical help in the Soviet Union.

The following encouraged me in my approach to the course, and were helpful in their appraisal of the general scheme: Tony Kingsford, David Hargreaves, James Nord, Bert Pockney and John Ross.

Jill Butler is hard-working, patient, kind and cheerful, and more than competent. My thanks to her, and to Vera Chalidze, who read the proofs.

Let's not forget Huw Davies the designer assisted by Peter Moore who had to make sense of it!

Cartoons by Harley Bishop
Maps on pages 64/5 and 80/1 by Hugh Ribbans

The cover photograph is reproduced by permission of ZEFA Picture Library (UK) Ltd.

The following photographs are reproduced by permission of NOVOSTI PRESS AGENCY:—Ice hockey page 8, ice hockey 4- & 6-year-olds page 20, sports—skaters page 20, Galina Kulakova page 20, football player page 19, Sultanbekov, war veteran page 19, tea-room page 37, Ikon page 78, market page 91.

The remaining photographs were taken for the BBC by Mary Sprent.